# *Nautch Boy*

## Also by the Author

*Lean Days*
*The Last Courtesan*

## Advance Praise for *Nautch Boy*

'Manish Gaekwad has produced a compelling sequel, *Nautch Boy*, to his daring effort to write the life and times of his mother as a tawaif, titled *The Last Courtesan: Writing My Mother's Memoir*. The genre of actual writings by courtesans is rare, maybe because publishers did not dare publish such works because of the prudery and hypocrisy of our middle class, which would have been their potential audience. Gaekwad's recollections paint an honest picture of the trials and tribulations of life in the kotha that strips off the glamour and romance in which courtesans' existence is couched in representations in most films. Here is a raw and direct depiction of an aspiring young writer and unwelcome son's life in the shadow of his mother's beleaguered life. Gaekwad's voice is candid and the portraits he creates of the mysteries of the kotha will disabuse many of their stereotypical understanding of a profession that enables the development of creative talent in its gifted denizens.'

—Veena Talwar Oldenburg

## Praise for *The Last Courtesan*

'*The Last Courtesan* is a one-of-a-kind book, not because it is the memoir of a courtesan, but because it is penned by her son, who was born in a kotha. I cried when I heard Manish speaking about his childhood at a literary event, visualizing a baby boy in a kotha, alone and aloof, and I cried even more when I actually read the book, terrified by the life of Rekhabai as a girl child trafficked and sold as a tawaif. It takes a ferocious spirit with incredible resilience to survive the saddest alleys of the world as traversed by Rekhabai as a tawaif and a mother, but it also takes an extraordinary man emancipated from the patriarchal social constructs of gender to narrate his mother's life as a tawaif with such nuanced perspective. It is an amazing book, which grows heavier and unsettling, and drowns you in helpless anguish and resentful grief about the countless little children and innocent young women who have lived and died as dehumanized tawaifs and sex workers, whose stories are untold, unwritten and thus unknown. I consider this book sacred. It is consecrated with my bleeding heart.'

— K.R. Meera

'*The Last Courtesan* is a book of violence, struggle ... almost a war, but with a lot of hope and enthusiasm towards life. This is a woman's struggle for existence, which translates to a journey of courage, intelligence, compassion and hope for the future. It is no ordinary book. And Rekhabai is no ordinary person.

'She is weak and strong, ferocious and gentle, angry and generous, with the power to take life into her hands in spite of the cruel world around her.

'Manish Gaekwad, without any fictionalizing intention and with a style as simple as his mother's heart and as complex as her life, has compelled us to read without a break.'

—Volga

'One outstanding book, this! Take a bow.'

—Anita Nair

'Writing about intimate, immediate relationships with distance and impartiality is like rubbing sandpaper on one's skin. Manish Gaekwad successfully does that to peel off the layers and show the socio-economic realities of a world rarely written about, in a smooth, authentic, forceful and intriguing way.'

—Neha Dixit

'Courtesans and dancing girls have long been the objects of fascination and opprobrium, and a great many books and films have featured and studied them. But it is very rare that they have been able to speak for themselves, or those who know them and their lives have written about them. *The Last Courtesan: Writing My Mother's Memoir* is one such work, which tells the story of Rekhabai, a courtesan in 1980s' Calcutta, an extraordinary individual whose life envelops barely known or ill-understood social histories of Hindustani music, kathak and some of India's most marginalized communities.'

—Anna Morcom

'The son's writing brings the struggles of a mother's life into memory with a swelling pain in the heart, speaking to the reader with complete honesty and without any concealment. It offers a resonance that speaks both to integrity and to literary quality.'

—Salma

'*The Last Courtesan* is a tribute to a dying culture and an undying ode to a loving mother. It is as deeply personal as it is emotionally resonant.'

—Kaveree Bamzai

'I'm not a great fan of memoirs, but I gobbled up *The Last Courtesan* in two days. Tenderly told with an evocative voice, this is a tribute by a son to his mother. Manish Gaekwad traces the tangled history of his mother's life with great courage, and masterfully captures her voice in his writing.'

—Tarana Husain Khan

'Not only is this memoir a beautiful retelling of an incredibly difficult and arduous life, it is also the story of a mother, a dutiful sister and a proficient courtesan. While it is a story of hardship, at all times, it also remains hopeful and optimistic, just like Rekhabai herself! Written with raw candour, the book also urgently throws light on the lives of marginalized people and on perhaps the most vulnerable tribes (here the Bedias and the Kanjar community) and how we, with our privileges, know so little about their lives. A must-read!'

—Nusrat Jafri

'A motherlode of a story.'

—Bina Nayak

'The eye-opening account of a brave courtesan, who had dreams like every other girl to support her family but was sold at a very tender age. Even as a child, she had a thinking mind, a spiritual quest. She was fearless in every situation, lived her life on her own terms and gave her son wings to fly and dream. In her memoir, she narrates her tumultuous journey to her writer son with sparkling honesty, an abundance of joy and an irrepressible spirit. A must-read!'

—Rekha Bhardwaj

'A heartbreaking testimonial by a son about his mother's exploitation. A must-read for those who want to understand the legacies of colonialism and sexism, especially among nomadic tribes.'

—Ruchira Gupta

'In *The Last Courtesan*, we learn not only about Rekhabai's life, but also about the tenacious and brittle world of the courtesans as it was finally crumbling under the pressures of a changing world that would now prefer glitzy dance bars to subtle charm. To say that Gaekwad had a complicated relationship with his free-spirited, occasionally trash-talking mother is an understatement. This is a haunting and haunted memoir, in which one senses the author's bated breath as he courageously bears witness to his mother's rage, her occasional helplessness, her fiery feminism and her lasting grace. With this bravura performance, Gaekwad has given his extraordinary mother a most precious gift—a voice—and continues to channel his own in *Nautch Boy.*'

—Ira Mukhoty

'Tumultuous and heart-warming.'

—BBC

'It's a book with a big heart and an expansive view of humanity.'

—*The Hindu*

'Irreverent, innovative, brutally honest and hugely compassionate, this memoir is compelling and unputdownable.'

—*The Telegraph*

'*The Last Courtesan* is a more contemporary story—a uniquely intimate memoir, told in first person in his mother's voice by author-journalist Manish Gaekwad.'

—*Mint Lounge*

'The book is more than just another narrative of resilience. Its shapeshifting journey cuts across major historical events and plays with a wide emotional spectrum. Further, it offers insights into the country's mujra culture. Rekha's story is perhaps the best argument to defend the claim that all stories matter. In her absence, her gritty stories come in handy to grieve her vibrant life. While her loss is irretrievable, it would have been a tremendous disservice to literature had Gaekwad decided against writing the book.'

—*The New Indian Express*

'Manish Gaekwad begins the book with, "I have entertained the thought of killing my mother", only to make her—an otherwise unknown woman from the many gullies and hovels that are invisible to most of us—come alive in these pages.'

—*Hindustan Times*

'*The Last Courtesan* unfolds with the flair of a 1980s' Bollywood action film, yet dives deeper, capturing Rekha Devi's resilience and artistry.'

—The Print

'An astute reminder of why we need to tell our stories.'

—*Business Standard*

'The book encapsulates a lifetime, but there is hardly a dull moment. It goes on at a pace, sometimes slow, sometimes fast—just like life itself. Only a tawaif's life pans out in a different space, a rare glimpse of which is this brave memoir.'

—*The Tribune*

'This is the story of a mother being narrated by the son, and the son decides to cut out the frills and opt for a real representation: sordid, grimy, depressing and yet sparklingly triumphant.'

—*Deccan Chronicle*

'This is an atmospheric story, and the one thing the reader takes away is how Rekha played the game of life adroitly, hard-headedly.'

—*Deccan Herald*

'*The Last Courtesan* [is] a heartfelt account of a tawaif's life that is filled with sorrow and pain, but nevertheless the story that becomes immortal is that of strength and grace, even in the face of extreme suffering and struggle.'

—*The Federal*

# *Nautch Boy*

*A memoir of my life in the kothas*

Manish Gaekwad

HarperCollins *Publishers* India

First published in English in India by HarperCollins *Publishers* 2025
HarperCollins *Publishers* India, Cyber City,
Building 10-A, Gurugram, Haryana-122002, India
www.harpercollins.co.in

2 4 6 8 10 9 7 5 3 1



P-ISBN: 978-93-6989-112-2
E-ISBN: 978-93-6989-350-8



Some names have been changed for legal reasons.



Typeset in 11.5/15.2 Adobe Garamond Pro
by HarperCollins *Publishers* India Pvt. Ltd

Printed and bound at
Thomson Press (India) Ltd

FSC
www.fsc.org
MIX
Paper | Supporting responsible forestry
FSC® C010615

This book is produced from independently certified FSC® paper to ensure responsible forest management.

HarperCollins *Publishers*, Macken House, 39/40 Mayor Street Upper, Dublin 1, D01 C9W8, Ireland

*For my mother, whose dance shaped my dreams*

# Introduction

My mother entertained the thought of killing me. A few hours before I was born. In the hierarchy of noble thoughts, I ranked second in priority. Her own life claimed the top spot—and with good reason: She had to survive before any of this, whether my story or even hers, was possible.

*Bachcha jaane do, mujhe bachaao,* she cried. Let go of the baby, save me.

To her credit, she did not use the more actionable words *bachcha maar do*. Kill the (damn) baby. She could not have possibly said that. Was her God testing her? Let go, as in let it slip away. *Jaane do.* A first-time mother—but a murderess? Oh no, she was incapable of that. No gestating mother wants to be a baby killer. But what if it involves a deliver-and-die scenario?

*Mujhe bachcha nahi chahiye*, she frantically repeated, trying to make herself heard loud and clear to the nurses treating her. I don't want the baby.

She was pleading mercy to the surgeon gods. She did not mean to kill the foetus. But in this dire situation, she did not want it, especially if saving it meant her own life would be exterminated.

She was being wheeled into the operation theatre for a messy delivery. She had overheard the lady doctor Bohra confide to a nurse that they would have to do a Caesarean. Cut her stomach into two and piece her back again, like an illusionist's trick. A normal delivery was ruled out. There was a high probability of losing one of us. Her pelvis was too fragile to push the baby out, her vagina too small to yawn or regurgitate it like a food disagreeable with her sensitive stomach. I had turtled and turned my face away inside her womb, unwilling to leave the comfort of the warm amniotic fluid I was floating in. She was in great pain—a scrawny young woman who was in the hospital for six months, carrying a foetus her body could not bear the weight of.

My *najayaz*, illegitimate, father, Rehmat Khan, used to visit her infrequently. His *chamcha*s, sycophant friends, visited my mother, filling her ears with gossip about how he frequented the kothas of other tawaifs in her long absence. *Woh Meena ke kothe pe hain. Woh Geeta ke kothe pe hain. Woh Malka ke kothe pe hain.* Rehmat Khan had quite the appetite for entertainment. Mother had not married him. Khan Saab, as she called him, was her patron in the kotha where she worked as a tawaif, performing mujras. They had quarrelled about the baby. She wanted it. He agreed for her to have it. But he wanted no other responsibility. He was already a family man with a wife in purdah and three happy children. They were clueless about his secret life in the kothas, or helpless, as most Indian households are when they discover their hostile dependency on a serial adulterer. *Main apna naam nahi de sakta,* he said. How could he give his name to a tawaif's child? *La haul bila kuat!* Ironic for a man whose name, Rehmat, means compassion, kindness, mercy.

His double standards aggravated her labour pain to a dirge she was singing at her own funeral.

My mother had conceived a baby because she wanted to get back at the sniggering tawaifs in the kotha who mocked her, calling her baanjh, infertile—a woman who would have no legacy. So she demanded a child when my father was courting her.

*Mujhe bachcha chahiye,* she tempestuously said to him one day.

It was an order, not a request.

She knew he was married. She had spent enough time in her profession to understand that no bachelor was going to arrive at her kotha with a colourful, noisily musical baraat. That is a rather early plug for the funereal but hopeful climax of *Pakeezah*, where Allama Iqbal's sher is aptly read aloud:

*Hazāroñ saal nargis apnī be-nūrī pe rotī hai*
*Baḍī mushkil se hotā hai chaman meñ dīda-var paidā.*

Unadmired, the narcissus weeps a thousand years
For an aesthete to cherish its inimitable beauty.

Miles from being an aesthete, my illegitimate father was only too happy to serve a challenge and perhaps prove his own worth. Patrons love flaunting their virility in a kotha where only a few get the opportunity of intimacy with a tawaif. It is unlike a brothel, where they can pay and have a limitless choice of sex workers to pick from.

A kotha is for entertainment. And to tawaifs, sex work is not entertaining. It is never part of their performance. Their mujra of song and dance is conducted in a mehfil, a gathering of several patrons. The patrons go back home to their wife and children, after kite-flying crisp currency notes for the tawaif's special attention—where they get a thenga, a wiggly thumb, for nothing in return. The tawaif chooses a patron she likes. Flashing money will not get her attention—as they say, tawaifs see more money falling at their feet each night than they see morals in the eyes of men truly valuing them. The lucky patron she picks can be her only one for as long as she wishes him to be—for a night, a week, months, years or even a lifetime, in some cases. Who am I fooling? No patron returns the loyalty back as favourably.

The tawaif can choose to have a child or not with her favoured patron. She is fortunate if that child is a girl, who can carry forward her name in the trade. But what about a boy? Turn him into a tabalchi, a tabla player, or any other musician—a baajawala or a sarangiwala. What use would such a child be in the world, my mother thought, if the foetus could not have its father's name in the likely event that its mother died in childbirth. Was there a more cursed life than to be born an orphan? She knew perfectly well how difficult it would be for me. She had seen a worse fate—as a child, she had been used to pay off a debt to a Bedia family, dressed as a child bride, raped by her husband and then sold to a kotha. When a family offered no guarantees, could one be better off without it?

No mother wants to give birth to an orphan.

The Caesarean was a success.

Dr Bohra dangled me by an ankle after cutting the bloody umbilical cord of uncertainty and said to my mother, *Dekho Rekha, ladka hua hai!* See, Rekha, you have a boy! My mother looked at me and fainted. She could not believe I was stubbornly alive. Like her. She had no energy left in her to remain conscious. She had prayed for a girl. Maybe the disappointment made her collapse. I was immediately put into an incubator.

When she woke up after two days, she asked the daiyya, midwife Pushpa, *Mera bachcha kahaan hai?* Where is my child?

Pushpa told her that I, a premature baby, was weak and had been kept under watch. A week passed. I was not shown to my mother. She panicked. She had a vision in her dream. The Sufi saint of Ajmer, Khwaja Moinuddin Chisti, and Goddess Kali instructed her to take her child away, or Yamraj, the God of Death, would do so. Yep, that sounds like the dance-off of the thunder-clapping gods.

Apparently, according to my mother, the morning I was born, there was a violent hurricane in Calcutta. *Bahut badaa toofan aaya tha*, she said with astounded eyes. As it so happens in every thunder and lightning oral story, which sounds as hokey as a Hindi-film flashback. *Achanak se kaale badal hatey aur tu subah ki pehli kiran jaise nikla.* You shot out like the first ray of dawn as the sun emerged from the dark clouds. Her ignoble thoughts may have been those nebulous clouds. Her sentiments, however, sweeten the comical.

Mother fought with the hospital staff, signed a patient's risk form and dashed out of the compound, hailing a taxi to take me home. She was an emotional heroine on the run from her well-wishers. The hospital staff was almost certain she was going to kill her baby. Her mother, Gullo, the tobacco-chewing hard nut of a woman who carried a sarota, nutcracker, in her ghagra, which doubled as a self-defence weapon, was waiting for her at the kotha. The staff had informed Gullo that Rekha would recover soon, but that the child's future was uncertain. Rekha would now have to dodge and survive the weaponized sarota flying through the kotha doors, risking even the newborn.

She pressed her infant tightly to her chest. Both of us breathless.

A Tawaif Smothers Her Newborn with Love. Killer headline in *The Telegraph*. I can rewrite my beginning as my end.

As thrilling as all of this sounds, I would have preferred to remain incubated in the hospital. She acted rashly in blind faith—no, actually, blinded by faith. I could have died. She almost killed me.

Twice.

But she gave me life instead. Twice as much. Hers and mine. Our resilient lives.

How did she intuit? Probably grasped from her own early experiences when life pushed her off the cliff. She found the courage and the derring-do to endure its twists and turns, like a fledgling songbird falling from its nest learns to soar before it touches the ground. No training, no practice, just killer instinct.

# Calcutta

VIOLENCE CREATES A MORE IMPRESSIONABLE MEMORY THAN LOVE.

When I run backwards into my barefooted childhood, I find that the only thing that threads together the series of events are sudden acts of violence and their irredeemable consequences. Acts of tenderness, love and care do not shine through the fog of memories. They must have been abundant and common. It is the violence that blazes through, like a red-hot stinging slap on the cheek for a harmless mischief. Or as an electric-blue thwack on the other set of rounded cheeks for a pardonable mistake.

First there was that violent birth, followed by the violence of my father Khan Saab snatching me from my mother when she boarded the train at Howrah station. She was heading to Bombay.

*Yeh mera bachcha hai,* he said. *Mera khoon hai.* My child, my blood.

He thought she would step down from the train. Snatching me would mean stalling her. The train stopped for no one. It began moving, slowly wheeling out of the platform with a whistle and a chug.

*Le lo,* she said. Take it. *Main aur paida kar loongi.* I can have more.

She was not being generous. She was calling his bluff. What would he do with an infant? Dump it on the railway tracks? Gift it to a destitute? Take it to his wife?

Hah!

She pretended indifference.

Khan Saab's friend Eshwar (let us take a moment here for his name, which translates as God, who serves as the deus ex machina) ran up to him and said, *Arre, yeh kya kar rahe hain aap?* What are you doing? What will you do with a child? This is a bad idea. You do not want this baby. You will have to put him in an orphanage. Is that what you want to do? Deny a child his mother?

The train picked up speed.

Mother watched me being separated from her. She felt her life flowing away in the opposite direction. Past her, as her past. Her heart sank, her body felt hollow. Her eyes welled up, but she did not budge. She would not give Khan Saab the satisfaction of seeing her break down. That would be his victory.

She was leaving the city, and him, because he had become a nuisance. He would arrive at the kotha during her mujra performances and disrupt it. She would be singing a standard song requested by a patron, like *Do Sitaron Ka Zameen Par Hai Milan Aaj Ki Raat.* Khan Saab would step in just as she was scaling the high notes of the lyrics, *Saari Duniya Nazar Aati Hai Dulhan Aaj Ki Raat.* Dulhan my foot! He would sneak into the adjacent room where I was sleeping and pinch my cheeks. My cries would interrupt her performance. He wanted her undivided attention by meddling with her work. Patrons got up and left. They did not come to the kotha to witness a fracas. A tawaif worked after putting her infant to sleep.

Or at least the visuals in the song *Jinhe Naaz Hai Hind Par Woh Kahan Hai* in *Pyaasa* made it de rigueur. Khan Saab heckled her. She locked the door. He banged. She told the dalaals, pimps, on the street to stop him. He shouted and created further embarrassment for her. Drunk, agitated, confusing lust with love, he was ruining her business.

Khan Saab now ran towards her at the station. She stood at the door of the moving train, frozen by the horror of her ordeal. She did not smile. He put me back in my mother's arms. She turned away from him and cried, kissing me repeatedly. *Mera bachcha, mera bachcha!* My son!

She did not turn to thank him or wish him goodbye. The train sped away. He was out of sight.

Past her, her past.

# Bombay

WHEN WE ARRIVED IN BOMBAY, MOTHER WORKED IN THE KOTHAS of Foras Road, primarily in the famously infamous kotha Bacchu Seth Ki Wadi located in Kamathipura, which was frequently haunted by such local dons as Haji Mastan, Dawood Ibrahim and Karim Lala. Mastan came with his girlfriends, she once said to me. Mother was in a new city. She had to reinvent herself. She rented a room in a building complex called Pavanpul on V.P. Road, close to the party office of the Indian National Congress. The kothas in Pavanpul were also loosely called the Congress House, with a similar hustle for primacy. Party workers were regular patrons. The compound housed the kothas under the entrance signboard of Bombay Sangeet Kalakar Mandal, an association formed by the tawaifs, who thought of themselves as performing artistes and did not want to be grouped with the sex workers of Foras Road in the Kamathipura area. In the after hours, when the security guard of Pavanpul blew a whistle to signal the closure of the entertainment hour, patrons had to exit the compound. Pavanpul was shut. The baijis then took a taxi to Foras Road, where the mujras continued until the morning azaan.

If you now look at the distance between Foras Road and Kamathipura on Google Maps, you will notice the road curving like a boomerang—which, once tossed, always returns, ironically, like the two professions that have coexisted in Kamathipura for long.

Mother was introduced to patrons as *Kalkatta ki mashoor dancer* Rekha Bai. Calcutta's famous dancer. That helped build curiosity around her, even if no one had seen or heard of her. The tawaif community was informed. When a saazinda, a musician, visited a kotha in a city, they carried gossip of who was flourishing elsewhere. My mother had proven her mettle in several kothas across Calcutta. Her fame had also travelled to Bombay before she did.

In the new kotha, Mother had to look after me, her own mother, her father, her sisters from Poona who came visiting, their children, cousins, relatives, friends of relatives—the whole village. They were enchanted by her glamorous-looking life of song and dance, sequinned saris, flashy jewellery, and exaggerated hair and make-up. But, essentially, they were around her for the money she distributed among them. She was a cash cow who could balance a bottle on her head and shake her hips to *Do Ghoont Mujhe Bhi Pila De Sharaabi*, looking part circus acrobat and part junior artiste in a Hindi film.

Several years ago, when Mother was a child, singing and dancing with her pet goat Neelkamal on the outskirts of Poona—where she lived in a hut with her mother Gullo, her father Tadiya, her six sisters (not counting the two others who died in infancy) and one brother—winning a lottery would not have improved their poor lives. What would they do after the money was over? Tadiya was a lowly security guard drunk on the job. He even got his name Tadiya from taadi, a desi daaru, country liquor he loved more than his family, so much so that even on his deathbed his last breath came after a final sip of the beloved alcohol administered by his dutiful wife Gullo. She had to fulfil his last wish. He could not live for it but would not die without it either. Gullo worked as a labourer in the crop fields, washing utensils at weddings and boiling goat-blood pudding when she could afford more than kaanji, rice water gruel, for her perpetually hungry children. When Gullo traded my mother, still a little girl, for a debt to a moneylender from the Bedia tribe whom she could not repay, the lender's family wedded my mother to their young son, took her to their home in Agra, made her work day and night for the family, and as she reached puberty, tried to sell her in Sonagachi, the red-light district in Calcutta. She was unsaleable. She was no longer a virgin. They settled for a kotha in Bowbazar, where mujras were performed. The Bedia family trafficked young girls. Mother took to the new environment without a fight—anything was better than to serve her husband's loathsome family. She arrived in the kotha with a bottle of lemon pickle, a period-stained skirt and a heart beating doubly loud—compacted from fear and excitement. Tired from a long train journey, she slept in the afternoon. When she woke up in the evening, the kotha was brimming with sounds of a tanpura and a shrill voice scaling the seven swars, notes. She heard a tabla, a baaja, a sarangi, ghungroo and giggles. She smelt fragrant flowers in the atmosphere. She saw incense smoke curls dancing in the air. She saw young girls dressed in shimmering clothes and jewellery, their faces powdered, their lips painted red. She was offered a cup of tea that she did not have to make. Her heart released from the tight clutch of her fears. She smiled. A first in many years. She felt free. She felt at home in this new environment—for a girl who had by now begun to understand she had no permanent home, she was learning to adjust and make any new nest her temporary home. She sipped her tea from the saucer, slurping to match the rhythm of her now bouncy heart. She no longer had to cook and clean for her tyrant mother-in-law. She no longer had to be raped by her husband. She knew it was rape—it was brute force, against her will. Mother looked innocent, but she was not naïve. She had to learn to sing the ghazals of Ghalib and Mir, and train in kathak with ustads, wear make-up, nice clothes, and observe the older girls who performed for patrons, sometimes sitting behind them to chorus. She was not sold to any patron, not abused, not beaten, not locked. She was now a free bird with clipped wings inside a menagerie. She pranced like her pet goat Neelkamal. As luck and hard work favoured my mother, in a few years she started doing well financially, escaped and traced her way back to the hut, told her family about her horrible time with the Bedias and gave her mother Gullo money. This is as close as it got to a lottery bonanza that Gullo would keep winning as long as Mother toiled in the kotha to keep her family away from debt and child trafficking.

This is her history in brief, preceding my memory.

Since memory is past us, it can appear to be a mirage, a lie. Memory to me feels like history in fiction. Does history exist outside memory? We step back in time to retell, and, sometimes, in doing so, the lights, shadows, colours and visuals can blur around the edges. We tell stories in ways that pale facts for fantasy. Was it real? Was it a dream? Should I believe everything my mother said to me about her past? She had no reason to lie. She had wanted to tell her story. In fact, I can recall my memory of her telling her story like it was yesterday. I was sitting at the door of her room in the kotha, where the sunlight fell in a fat, white beam. I was doing my homework. My mother was sitting in the next room's door, where another fat, white beam fell. We could see each other straight across. The sliding door between the two small rooms was wide open. She had no make-up on, her frizzy, curly hair was loose and she was fiddling with a tape recorder. There was a gigantic tanpura behind her. She would often play it after a bath, dressed in a white sari, trying to pass off as the goddess of music, Saraswati. Mother looked like a vision, I will give her that. That is why that image of her persists in my memory. I saw her inserting an audio cassette into a National Panasonic tape recorder, and recording herself talking. She looked at me and said, *Yeh main tere liye kar rahi hoon, taaki tu meri kahani jaan sakey.* I am doing this for you to know my story. I must have been eight or nine then. At that age, I was more attentive to my books than her sharp, high-pitched voice, which was white noise in the background then, as it still is in rewind.

It was only in 2020, some thirty-odd years later, when we started discussing the idea of writing her memoir that I asked about the audio cassette. She had lost it in moving from the closed kotha to her new flat. She was in her final years when we sat to record her memories on my phone. Memory is hazy, and in the telling, appears fantastical, but she knew one of her own siblings would be able to corroborate her story. I spoke to her sisters. What they said was ironic. Beauty spoils upon touch. She paid a price for her beauty and innocence, which the other sisters lacked. They were all lined up for the Bedia family to choose from, but it was my mother who was picked—a raggedy doll with a sparkly smile. I can picture her holding a thin crook to guide her goat Neelkamal on a pasture. An unlucky day for her, but a meal ticket for her family. She changed their lives for the better with her cursed fate as it landed in her own two tiny hands. She was never told why she was picked. She probably felt the most wretched, unloved. Had she known she was beautiful, maybe her story would have ended sooner than she got a chance to change her destiny. Her lack of vanity also perhaps helped her survive a reasonably long career as a tawaif—some twenty-odd years, before the culture faded out in the mid-Nineties, putting her out of work.

In the kotha, beauty soon becomes its own enemy, as was the case she often told me about her cousin sister Hasina, ironically both by her beautiful name and ghamand, hubris. She said to my mother, *Didi, aap toh khamakha itna mehnat karti hain. Mujhe dekhiye, yeh saara khel meri aankhon ka hain.* Sister, you work too hard. Look at me, it is all a game I command with my eyes. Beshaq, my mother thought, without a doubt. She mesmerized men. Hasina had almond-shaped, big, hazel-brown, cat-like eyes filled with lust for the good life without the hard work. *Kanji aankhein,* said Mother. Hasina did not excel at singing or dancing, but had dreams of becoming a movie star, willing to cozy up to goons, a gutka baron and even a soundman on film. I had met two of these men in my teens. The sound uncle took me to Esel Studio for a C-grade film shoot where a woman, not Hasina Aunty, is molested by a bunch of hoodlums in a stormy and thunderous temple. I was disturbed by how physically violent the men were. The woman did not seem to object. It was rough. Another time, the portly gutka baron uncle took Hasina Aunty and me for a weekend vacation to Mahabaleshwar. I can attest that at both times I felt that Hasina Aunty was struggling to juggle these two men, her beauty replaced by its illusion to hold on steadfast as they treated her only as a distraction from their more stable family lives.

As a child being raised in a kotha in Bombay, I see myself, a toddler walking with Mother on Kennedy Bridge, holding her hand, looking at her smiling reflection in puddles of rainwater and staring back at her, wondering how she was present in it. She was the rain, and if I looked up, she was the moon. I was puzzled. How was this angelic woman's face in everything I saw?

I remember a horse ride on the Chowpatty. The horse trainer held the white beast by a rope and ran alongside, saying we had to run fast. There was a trophy at the end of the beach, a clock. Ghadi, he said. Did he mean ghadi as a clock or as this moment? Ghadi-ghadi he says ghadi. This memory has no end. We gallop to the tick-tock sounds of the horse shoes or the sound of the needles tick-tocking on the clock? It sounds like a surreal dream.

I remember a patron, Qamar Uncle, who took me shopping, bought a number of women's shiny shoes in red, black and white, and gave me lots of chocolate. Foreign brands, such as the pyramid-shaped Toblerone. He was from Oman. I do not remember who got those shoes. Maybe the chocolates were a sweet distraction to impress my mother with his gifts.

But, most importantly, I remember the violence of crying. My memory of it has a dream-like patina, notoriously involving Mother and one of her tawaif friends resisting a ruffian in a noisy scuffle. I see a flashy knife, her severed finger and blood on the dance floor. I bawled so hard in the arms of a girl holding me in the corridor at the top of the creaky wooden staircase. I stretched out my arm to reach Mother. It remains my first flashback. A clear, restored black-and-white print, crisp as an autumn leaf. And yet it threatens to speed up into a gauzy, poor-quality spool tape when I retrace. Fading away, like the charring edges of a shakily shot silent film.

Fire and havoc play a part outside the edges of memory. Once, in a fire in the kotha, Mother's younger sister Shanna escaped with me in her arms. Mother was trapped on the terrace of the building, worried about me, but also relieved to spot Shanna waving and shouting at her, *Didi, hum theek hain.* Sister, we are fine. Another time a manservant drugged Ashok, a relative who was babysitting me, while Mother was away for a performance. When she returned, she found him unconscious, locked in her room from the inside. She had to break the door as I was also inside, wailing. I responded to her when she spoke to me through the keyhole to get away from the door. *Darwaze se hatt ja, beta,* she said. Her voice was attracting me, unbeknownst, towards a melodious violence. As an infant, I did not understand it was a warning. It sounded sweet as music, familiar in her soft, nurturing tone.

Mother said we had to leave Bombay in a hurry. Two goons were fighting for Hasina Aunty's hand. They wanted Mother's permission to marry her. They did not need it. They flashed knives, pistols, threatened to kidnap me from a nearby crèche. They just wanted to scare Mother to choose between the lesser evil of the two unsuitable suitors for her cousin sister. Didi, they teased her, dripping with sarcasm. Do the right thing, they laughed. Mother was scared, but fear made her brittle. She kept her calm, not riling the prospective grooms. She could not let this mess squander my chances at a better life. Mother asked both interested parties to come back at a later date. They took her word. Finding herself cornered, she could still avoid a catastrophe with her conviction—an artful wave of her dancing hand, a naughty smile, a complicit wink. She managed to escape, returning to Calcutta.

# Bengal

Violence, even when not physical, is agonizing and hurtful—like the time I felt abandoned and orphaned when my mother admitted me into a boarding school, far, far away from her. I was seven when I felt stranded, alone and cold in the wintry weather of Darjeeling. This was not the first time she had left me, but it felt like the first betrayal. I had started thinking for myself by then. Why was she leaving me here? When would I see her again?

*Acche se rehna, haan,* she said. Stay well. I nodded. What else was there to say? Bye, she said. She wept. I wept. But now, when I jog back, I had asked for it. She had put me in the Little Flower Boarding School in Kurseong when I was five. I do not recollect that particular goodbye. She had just returned to Calcutta from Bombay and was advised by her Masterji, who taught her how to read and write in Hindi at the kotha, to put me in a boarding school in the hills for my safety and better education. The kotha was not ideal or safe. Mother did not dither. Lots of tawaifs before her had done the same. The Kurseong school was only till Class 2. When it was time to leave, Mother asked me, Where do you want to study? Darjeeling, I said, spelling out each letter: D A R J E E L I N G to impress her, lifting my tiny feet encased in shiny black leather Bata school shoes, holding the pleats of her lightly scented cream and blue chiffon sari and sweetly pleading her to take me where the toy train had once taken us kids for a picnic.

What was my life before the picnic?

What I remember most vividly about the Kurseong boarding school is that I was in the sick room with the other jailed inmates, where children with fevers or other less-severe illnesses like pretence, were quarantined. A girl my age asked, Can I sleep with you? Let us also establish our ages here. We were five and six, respectfully. I think. She had a trunkful of toys. Barbie dolls. Why would I say no to her? I climbed to the top of an empty bunk bed, and sang, *I Am a Disco Dancer*. Now, I do not recall why I did that. Show-off! She must have asked me to show a talent I have. I had laughed and started shaking my hips while standing on the wooden plank. It collapsed. I fell down on the lower bunk, which was, thankfully, cushioned. The next thing I knew, the principal was caning me for bad behaviour. Was it not nasty of him to beat a sick child? That night I went back to my bunk, stared at the full moon outside the window and howled. Another time, two inmates—a friend and I—forgot our school bags in class and decided to fetch it in the dark. We went down what seemed like a dank serpent's lair of a spiral staircase and peeped in through the glass door of the locked classroom, using our stubby hands as blinkers. We imagined the reflection of our own eyes as the eyes of a child-devouring monster staring back at us from inside the empty room. We screamed, knocked our heads accidently, violently, and scurried for our lives. Yet another time, a mad man entered the school and chased the children around. Screaming and yelling, the children were secured into the dining hall. When the mad man tried to peep in through the keyhole in the wooden door, some kid poked him in the eye with a fork that had only one prong. More screams followed on both sides. The door shook like a curtain in a storm of shrieks. Violence spawned violence. When a kid pushed me in class, I hid behind a door to slam it in his face. We were both caned. When I jokingly pushed a rusty, old wobbly slider in the playground, the PT teacher slapped me so hard I, too, fell with a loud thud, just like the tiny, dumb slider with feeble toes. Violence was rampant and unjust. When I fell on the playground and there was no Mother to kiss my bruised knee, would the wound heal quickly? I must have stifled my own cries, knowing there was no one to hear and hug me. That is also just me letting off steam in my attempt to come across as an early-onset drama queen. Boarding made us tough even before we learnt how to spell it. Or maybe the Jackie Chan action films shown to us on the weekends that looked harmless and comical, like *Tom and Jerry*, hollowed out our emotional responses. Violence only spun more untreated memories.

There was, however, one time when I may have tried to kill myself. Okay, kill is an innocuous word for a six-year-old. We try to kill ants by burying them in the garden soil. They still escape. I had the weapon—chocolate. I chewed so many candies that my jaw split from the exertion. One morning, when the kids had lined up for roll call, I was missing. The principal went looking for me in the dormitory and pulled back my quilt to find blood spilling from one side of my face. I was unconscious, or let us say asleep, to sound less dramatic. He picked me up in his arms and ran across the street in his red silk night robe to a hospital opposite our school. My left jaw was stitched back. When I woke up, I found my mother sitting by my bed. She had brought apples. Until then, only witches brought apples for the sick. And banana, and oranges, for a slack-jawed chimp like me, who could not chew apple at the time. I looked out of the window, smiling and waving at my friends, who were by now marching in line towards their classroom. I was happy to be sick. Happy to wave back vigorously at my friends waving at me, oblivious of my good luck even in the face of violence.

When she was in Darjeeling, Mother visited St. Paul's school. She was impressed by the sheer size of the building, but also intimidated that her small, frail, quiet and shy child would get lost in that sprawling space. She saw boys playing football and volleyball in the playground. They were big and loud. There were no girls around. It was an all-boys' school and the hostel fees were steep. She made her way out and reached another school, Daffodils. The school had a wooden exterior, which made it look cozy, tiny and hand-made, compared to St. Paul's imposing edifice in brick and stone. She found Daffodils homely. She watched young girls and boys play in a much smaller field. She felt comfortable. It looked like the school was managed more intimately than the booming hallways and corridors of St. Paul's, run by a rector she timidly addressed as Fatherji.

Watching my mother walk down the steep slope of the new boarding school in Darjeeling, her silhouette disappearing in the mist, I sat on a rocky mound, looking across at the Kanchenjunga, like it was the mountain in Toblerone. Looming mountains, a deep plunge of the valleys and the fog in the air—a sense of being lost overwhelmed me. These are not my words from back then, but from now when I think about it. Stillness stood before me. In Caspar David Friedrich's nineteenth-century painting *Wanderer above the Sea of Fog*, a formidable man looks admiringly beyond the clouds. I was the child version of that valiant man, sitting on a rocky precipice, looking at my uncertain future clouding in the mist.

I ran up a flight of stairs to a dormitory, tried reaching the latch of a window to see if I could open it to catch a final glimpse of Mother being ghoulishly swallowed by the mist.

Could you please help me? I asked a teacher who was walking by.

She opened the window for me. The fresh air revived me. I waved to Mother. She was gone, but a new knowledge was beginning to sink in. I was not alone. The teacher had helped me. The smiling, young face of a beautiful English teacher was replacing the violent act of my mother leaving me behind. Not everyone responded to me with violence.

Once a year, I returned home to the kotha in Bowbazar, Calcutta. The kotha, an unpainted, neglected house, stands as a cul-de-sac in Bandook Gully. Gun Lane—what a violent name for a place that fired sweet melodies for bullets. A thick iron gate guards the entrance. Rusty and unremarkable. No address, no fairy lights, not even a bell. As if only the spectre of the kotha exists. A haud, a mini well, is situated next to the entrance, from which water is collected twice a day at a designated hour. It leads to a small courtyard flanked by rooms on all sides, a common loo and a bathroom. An arch on the left leads to stairs going up a hallway with two rooms. The hallway has another set of stairs at the far end leading to another area called the chhata, the terrace, where new rooms are built to accommodate new tawaifs. Three long and narrow tin-roof kitchens stand on the left of the landing. Food is prepared on coals, or ghaaslet, kerosene oil. Gas arrived much later. Two people standing in the kitchen are a crowd. Their colliding shadows block the light at the door, stuffing the room. A dalaan, space in the centre of the chhata, gives the area some breathing room and light, with other rooms encircling it. A common loo and a bathroom are tucked away in the arch at the other end. One yellow bulb from the ceiling lights up both these spaces divided by a wall that does not reach the ceiling. A small iron bucket is kept outside the toilet, which needs to be filled with water for washing. There are no taps. No running water. Water is stored in a stout iron tank outside the kitchen, where utensils are washed. There are five rooms on the terrace. Each room is big enough to accommodate a tawaif's family, no matter the size, but too small for anything more than a party of five when patrons throng the kotha in the evenings. It is not all chandeliers and rose water, like *Pakeezah*. Sorry about repeating that reference. This film is as removed from reality as it is joyous to watch.

Memory is a CCTV camera into the past and can sometimes behave erratically, like the night-vision found footage in *The Blair Witch Project*. My memory invokes the kotha more as a horror-film set—colourless, dark, grim and filled with dead air.

My mother had a room and a half, partitioned by a dark brown (cockroach colour, I thought back then) wood panelling with opaque ribbed glass on top to filter light into the smaller one. The half-room functioned more like a storeroom, where members of her family stockpiled in the evenings. The big room opened to a window opposite it. The tall window had thick iron bars like a jail cell. It had no view. The ugly grey wall of another building blocked any air that tried to squeeze in through them. The window became illusory. A Banksy joke. A battery-operated black Bush radio with a spiry antenna sat on the window, a singing mynah in a cage. The top half of the big room was wallpapered in mustard yellow and red flowers. The brown panelling—or wainscoting—also skirted the lower half of the room. A square white gaddi was laid on one side with white bolsters. An oblong Belgian mirror at half tilt hung above it, giving my mother a clear view of her patron's head of hair during a mujra. A bald pate or a wig could be spotted in it. Spotting a man by his wig made it easier to loosen his wallet. He was more likely to enjoy personal attention. The mirror had a carved wooden frame of flowers painted in burnished gold that made the tawaif and her musicians look regal in its reflection. A musical painting. The floor was covered in a Rexine sheet with a chessboard pattern.

My mother sat on the floor to perform, taking the centre spot in the room, a queen in the game of pawns. The partition panel had pictures of deities such as Krishna (painted blue, coy and effete),

Laxmi, Saraswati, Kali and a photo of the Ajmer dargah high up, almost touching the ceiling and hooked at half tilt, as if the gods were looking down and blessing the mujra. Mother stood on a wooden stool to garland these deities with marigold, red hibiscus, rose, tuberose and jasmine flowers. The room smelt of incense sticks spreading strong floral scents in the morning. There were two or three khaats, wooden cots, in the dalaan. The afternoon hours were quiet during the women's siesta. A few girls played quietly with their dolls on the khaats. Boys were out in the thin gully, playing cricket. I played with the girls' toys. I did not have any toys in particular. Oh no, I was not that sad child without toys—it is just that I did not want the toys that boys played with: cars, guns, bats and balls. I never asked my mother for a toy. Once, when we were walking back home from the market, I saw a gas-balloon seller and insisted on one. A red one. Mummy, balloon! I pointed at the messenger of my wishes. She tugged at me to keep walking. I threw a fit. Mummy, balloon! I cried. She slapped me. In public. I was stunned into silence. After that, I never asked her for anything. Picture this moment as a Banksy mural of the girl with her red balloon going pop!

Violence muted my voice.

At sunset, the kotha transformed into a musical stage. In each room, a woman engaged in pooja or shringar, make-up. Bells clanged; the thick white smoke of lobaan perfumed the air. Lobaan was burnt in a lamp and carried to all corners of the room to purify the air and welcome visitors into a scented and soothing ambience. The silvery sounds of payal, the soapy smell of freshly shampooed hair with shikakai and amla, the rustle of shimmering silk fabrics and powdery eyelashes. The vocals of singers tuning with a baaja, the sarangiwala fixing the bolts in his femur-like musical instrument in the dalaan, the tablawala pulling the sides of the bloated skin on the drum. Soon the carnival barkers arrived—the phoolwala, the chana-badamwala, the paanwala, the phuchkawala, the phalwala—men with sharp voices that cut across the dulcet tones rising in the golden hue of yellow light bulbs switched on outside each room, as if to indicate they were now open for business. The kotha lit up like an all-night industrial park, with workers perfecting their instruments, preparing to cut a product into shape. The main gate lit up, the patrons walked in, guided by a pimp. The patrons in safari suits and dhoti-kurtas, unbeknownst to them, were the main products to be sized in half—by their wallets, at the very least.

I watched my mother apply foundation, rouge and red lipstick. She had a vanity box with all sorts of colourful powders, like a painter's palette. Puffs, brushes, kajal, bindi, payal, earrings, finger rings, toe rings, haath phool, maang tika, jhoomar, kamarband, baajuband, necklaces and nosepins sprung out of a lower compartment—to me a magician's hat, really. I could keel over if my curiosity was not contained. *Yeh kya hai, yeh kya hai?* I often pried. What is this? What is that? *Tere kaam ki cheez nahi hai, jaa apni kitaab padh,* Mother would say. Nothing for you to be interested in, go read your book.

She chose yellow glass bangles that evening. A maid combed her hair and adorned it with mogra flowers and a matching yellow chutila or chuttiya. Funny, this word, both in sound and letter, mimicking that cuss word. Chuttiya, I figured out a few years later, was a paranda, a hair adornment of silk threads and tassels. Paranda is a Punjabi word. I picked it up from the lyrics of the song *Kaali Teri Choti Hai, Paranda Tera Laal Ni.* In the kotha, the paranda was pleated into the choti, braid, and was called chuttiya, part of the braid. My mother then wore a gauzy yellow-gold lehenga embroidered in teeny-tiny silver bells. When she swirled, the bells danced to the music of her hips, producing the cascading sound of a waterfall. I was enraptured. I thought she was a hoor, a pari, an angel, who at times disappeared from the kotha at midnight, returned in the wee hours of the morning and tossed a bouquet of flowers on the bed where I slept. I woke up to the strong, sweet fragrance of rajnigandha in the room. I posed with the bouquet in the mirror. As if she had won an award and it was now in my care. I was proud of her. I plucked the plumpest red roses and arranged them in a vase on the windowsill without a view, as if we were immured behind it. Suffice it to say here that the entombment of Anarkali in *Mughal-E-Azam*, a film I watched in the kotha, always felt closer to our own harsh reality. It stoked the fire in our hearts to live just as defiantly and with our heads held high, at least within the four walls of the kotha that was built in such a way that it did not have a view of the world outside. There was a piece of sky overhead, through which light poured in, and the grey, unpainted cemented ground beneath our feet. We straddled this space like frogs in a deep, dark and dank well, albeit singing and dancing instead of croaking, as if to perfect the illusion. No birds descended. As if they, too, knew it was a trap. Leftover rice and shredded rotis were tossed on the tin roof of the kitchen. It was the only way to attract crows noisily hopping on it at dawn, giving the kotha the semblance of a lived space by day.

Where did you perform today? I asked my mother when she got back home just before dawn.

On stage, at a function for the police, she said.

Did you win the first prize?

Yes.

She did not show me her winning moves. She did not dance for me. She considered it inappropriate to entertain me. She did not want to influence me in any way; nurturing a talent in the performing arts would be digressing from her efforts to educate and secure a more stable future for me. She never asked me to sing or dance, but hearing how terrific she was on stage, how I wished I could watch her, how I wished I could be like her.

She gave me a bundle of crisp five-rupee notes, the kind that came directly from the bank to the kotha through eager, likely wigged patrons wanting to impress. It smelt as fresh as newly baked pound roti. Men of all shapes, sizes and promises came to see my mother's mujra. They earned quaint sobriquets derived from their personalities. Ungliwala, for poking his fingers in private matters; Bangali Babu, for speaking in the local language; Bakbakiya, for non-stop chatting. Chapadganju, Totaram and Kanjoosmakkhi were some of the others. They came chewing paan, talking gregariously, drinking fast, smoking furiously, clapping hard, singing along and some even getting up to dance. That was always more fun to watch and laugh at, because none of them were a match. Patrons screamed and shouted yelps of delight during a performance. Money floated in the air. It settled like dust around my mother. The walls of the kotha rooms were so thin that at times it was hard to tell one tune from the other when another performance was under way. Tricky to catch one singer from the other, their voices indistinct, melodies blending, saris and ghagras twirling in vigorous dance moves, the metallic sound of ghungroos creating a rhythm that put them in a trance. In this concatenation of ecstasies, a child peeping into a room wished a two-rupee note would fall closer to the purdah. It made stealing a natural second component of our own make-up. The first being sneaky.

I watched patrons through the purdah, sometimes scratching a hole into its shiny fabric. Children were forbidden to enter the room a tawaif was performing in. A heavy jacquard purdah was dropped at the door when it was engaged. Children hung around the door, waiting for the manservant to arrive carrying a tray of alcohol, Thums Up, chana badam, potato chips, an ice bucket, soda, paan and water. The children pestered the attendant to give them a few peanuts.

*Baad mein!* Later! He shooed them away.

The children would often mess up the tray during a fight to grab a snack. Kids would peep in to see which patron was drinking how much of the Thums Up. They would gossip among themselves, choosing whose leftovers they would grab when the patrons exited the room. With a handful of nuts and half a bottle of soda in hand, the children felt like they had won a competition. I never participated in this game. If a servant handed me a bottle, I accepted it with reluctance, but never sipped directly from it. I would fetch an unused straw, and only then would it be acceptable for me to drink a stranger's leftovers. I also had to be careful not to be caught in the act by my mother. She did not approve of the servants giving me a patron's jhootha. She did not want their rank breath to reach my lips.

At midnight, when a security guard at the entrance blew a whistle, the patrons left in fits and starts. The musicians left satisfied, taking along their pay for the evening's performance. Before the evening started, at sunset, they would sit at the tea stalls along the tramline, smoking and awaiting an invite from a baiji. They were the daily-wage labourers of the mujra. The tawaifs stowed their earnings and carried their heated kadhaai steaming with chicken and mutton curry to one of their rooms, sharing their dinner. The servants sat along and ate together on the floor mats, laughing and gossiping about the evening's shindig. The children played with their food in the room heavily scented with mogra and sweat, tobacco and whisky.

Rajjo and Laxmi Aunty, my mother's cousins, lived with her for a few years. They looked after me. They sang *Re Mama Re Mama Re* to me as a lullaby. They were not good singers. They entertained patrons as chorus girls, sitting behind my mother during her mujras, accompanying her with claps and shrill vocals, singing *Tumko Piya Dil Diya Kitne Naaz Se*. The aunties took me to the cinema halls—Majestic, Crown, Hind, Orient, Paradise, Globe,

Elite, Jyoti, Roxy and Metro—when my mother was performing. Hindi films were their own kind of dark-room mujra, a grander spectacle where people clapped, sang, danced and threw money at the screen, just like they did at the kotha, showering the on-screen performers with their love and adulation. We watched old hits such as *Taj Mahal*, *Loafer*, *Anmol Moti* (billed as India's first underwater movie) and newer ones such as *Loha*, *Paap Ko Jala Kar Raakh Kar Doonga*, *Coolie*, *Hero* and *Pyar Jhukta Nahin* (someone said I looked like the kid in the film who reunites his estranged parents, which made me bawl a little more than the film merited). When Kavita Krishnamurthy playbacks in the song *Tum Se Mil Kar* filmed on the kid, she sings the lyrics *Maa, o maa, main tere dil mein hoon ke nahin hoon, tu toh meri nas nas mein basee hai.* O Mother, whether I am in your heart or not, you course through my veins. The words stung my heart. I wept throughout the film as if someone was separating me from my own mother. She was performing at the kotha, so perhaps it was her absence that tormented me during the film. Why was she not here, with us, watching this film together?

Mother's singing voice was sharp, thin and almost shrill, like a hawker selling her wares in a crowded town square. It stung the ear when she pitched high, though her patrons loved it. It did not captivate my heart like Krishnamurthy, who had a nasal, reedy timbre, which somehow sounded more musical even when she scaled up. On New Year's Eve, Doordarshan aired a special programme with singers, dancers and actors performing. It was the only way to see how my favourite singer looked. I stayed up till midnight, excited. Mother pointed to her and said, *Yeh hai teri Kavita.* This is your Kavita. Krishnamurthy was singing *Bijlee Girane Main Hoon Aayi. Yeh kaali kalooti?* some kid in the room said and laughed. This black girl? The comment was meant to mock my choice. It took me a second to grasp the insult. Her buckteeth briefly reminded me of Big Ethel in *The Archies* comics, but her beautiful voice quickly overshadowed the thought. Looks were secondary. My mother was beautiful by conventional standards—fair and tall—but her voice was no match. Krishnamurthy was a classically trained vocal artiste. Mother could dance phenomenally. Krishnamurthy gently swayed to her cadence. That did not change my opinion about where each one's strength lay. I clapped and sang along with Krishnamurthy.

Another film around the same time, *Kaash*, featured an estranged couple and a child, who was a mute spectator. Again, I was told I looked like the kid. These two films deeply affected me, enough to want to see the on-screen couple united and happy, subconsciously working on my latent desire to see my parents together. The aunties did not take me to Lighthouse, New Empire and Chaplin as they mainly played English films in those days. These were cinema halls I went to later as a teenager to watch adult films.

Some days, when the baijis were not performing on a festive occasion, the kids gathered in the tawaif Meena's room next door. She had a television, a VCR and even a telephone. A video-cassettewala used to come around with a duffel bag, renting out Bombino, Indus or Time–labelled Hindi titles at ten rupees and English ones for twenty. Pakistani stage plays such as *Buddha Ghar Pe Hai*, *Bakra Qiston Pe* and *Nach Meri Bulbul* were in high demand. Meena was our Jaya Prada. She looked and dressed immaculately, in matching saris, make-up and accessories, like the heroine of those Jaya–Sridevi-starrers. She loved hosting movie nights when the kids were over from the boarding for our winter vacation.

On one such cold night the tawaifs decided to watch *The Exorcist*, showing it to us kids too, who must have been scarred in different ways. There was a rumour in those days that some people had died watching it. No one in the kotha read the newspaper, so we did not know the source or authenticity of this. Meena loved sensational stuff. I suspect the tawaifs wanted to prove that nothing scared them. They had outlived worse horrors. They did not bat an eyelid. Meena put the video cassette into the VCR. Someone switched off the light. Gundi, Bunny, Gudiya and I huddled inside a razaai, quilt, and tried to peep only when the screen was quiet. I had zombie eyes by the end of it. No wonder my memory recalls the kotha as a haunted house.

Later, Rajjo Aunty ran away with a patron. Laxmi Aunty went to the Sealdah railway station and disappeared. This was not immediately after watching *The Exorcist*, but it was somewhere around that time. I am not correlating the two. It is just that in retrospect it feels as if the two aunties exorcized the nasha, intoxication, of becoming successful like my mother. Reality sunk its poisoned fangs deep into them. Mother did not despair when people abandoned her, but it was not to be so in my case.

One morning, a girl was combing Mother's curly hair in the sun. The kotha's famous qawwala Mallika Aapa's servant, Buddhu, asked me if I wanted to come with him to the market.

*Mummy, main bahar jaoon?* Can I go out? I asked my mother.

Hmm, she said, not turning to look at me.

I walked out of the kotha. Buddhu carried me on his shoulders, and hours went by with us wandering around the market, laughing and roaming around like urchins.

Where is my child? Mother suddenly began looking for me. She had forgotten that she had given me permission to step out. When I returned on Buddhu's shoulders, she looked worried. She beat me with the comb.

Where did you go? Why did you go? Who gave you permission? She yelled and spanked me.

I was puzzled. She was hitting me for no fault of mine. She scolded Buddhu. Buddhu was stupid. He never talked back. Violence was a form of care and protection for my mother. I was too young to understand her paranoia. My mother had fled Bombay for my safety. It haunted her. She forbade me from stepping out. She did not give me a reason.

Inside the kotha, playtime meant piling bolsters up on a gaddi, a teetering Jenga tower I would leap from, giggling as it swayed. Hide-and-seek was a different magic. Mother would sweep me under her petticoat, into a snug, shadowed world. There, a sharp, hot scent bloomed—something wild, like wet petals releasing a warm vapour that had a sour tang. It twisted my stomach, and I felt a queasy pull. When she tried to hide me there again, I wriggled free, unwilling to sink back into that secret place.

She had showed me a long, winding, surgical scar on her tummy. It looked liked the swollen welt from a whiplash, disappearing like a snake into a burrow. *Dekh, tu yahan se aaya hai,* she said. Look, this is where you have come from. I touched the soft, raised seam. My flesh goosed. I knew this river flowed down to where a dark, tangled thicket grew. I had glimpsed it once when she bathed me with her. Her body an open story, a map I could not decipher. That tufted nest—wild and mysterious … Was that where I had begun? The thought hummed in me, half-wonder, half-dread.

The little girls—Bansuri, Gundi, Gudiya and Munmun—were my only friends at the kotha when I returned home for the winters. We played with the kitchen set, the doctor set and the dollhouse. I am trying to make this bit sound as drab and ordinary as any queer child's story, which it usually is in the beginning, as these playtime signs are very clear indicators, often overlooked, but it may also not necessarily be obvious to all queer kids. Maybe it was the maahaul, environment, I grew up in. But then what about the other boys who did not play with the girls? Not every boy who grows up in a kotha becomes a tawaif. It is not the same for the girls either. Some girls get into sex work and some even find marriage—but the likelihood of the girls breaking out of the kotha into mainstream society is a lot lower than for a boy to shed his queerness. A boy's masculinity can become a curse, but his femininity is never a blessing. I had to balance the two.

Unfortunately, my mother, and the other tawaifs who saw the signs, did not try to fix it to return me to the secure folds of heteronormal masculine behaviour. They viewed it as a phase that I would outgrow. *Bachcha hi toh hai!* He is just a kid! Also, a word about the girl Gundi. As you can probably guess from her violently badass name, she was the rebellious one. She dressed like a boy, in a shirt, trousers and a waistcoat, kept her hair short and played cricket with the boys. She hated being told to practise singing and dancing, and would not wear ghungroos. What do you want to do, then? The baijis asked her. Fight, she said, clenching her fists and punching the air. She cut a picture of a rather beautiful boxer. She was a fair, pretty girl. Perfect for a tawaif's job. But she had other plans. I do not know what became of her after her aunt Meena left the kotha, returning the girl to her mother in a village in Agra. She was as unlikely to become a tawaif as I was dreaming of being one myself.

Mother bought a flat near New Market. She sent me there with Laxmi or Rajjo Aunty in the evening. She did not want me being seen by the men visiting the kotha at that hour. Patrons do not care for the children, but a cautious tawaif is better than a callow mother inside these crumbling walls, where nothing is certain—a convivial ambience can turn into a battleground without a warning if two drunk patrons get into a brawl over whose song request should be entertained first. Police arrive to disperse petty fights that sometimes involve bottles smashing and footwear flying. Catfights are a common sight during the day, but watching men and women slug it out with hair-pulling and blouse-ripping feels like an extreme sport of passion during the night. Between the screaming and the shouting, there is the violence of words. A torrent of cuss words. Madarchod. Madarchut. Behenchod. Behen Ki Chut. Randi. Raand. Khaangi. Bhadwa. Dalla. Gaandu. Chodu. Chodumal.

Chutiya. Chut Ka Jhaant. Chut Ki Khaal. Jhaantu. Lund Fakir. Bhosadi. Bhosada. Bhosadchod. Haramzada. Haramkhor. Harami. Bhaadkhau. Laundiyabaaz. Kutte Ka Pilla. Suar Ka Bachcha. Suar Ki Aulaad.

Missiles in my ears.

Children become traumatized receptacles of violent memory. *Kha kasam*, promise me, my mother said. *Meri kasam kha tu aisi zaban katai bhi istimaal nahi karega*. Swear on me you will never use such profane language. She had just finished a bout of sparring words with the huffy tawaif Phullo. I looked at her and nodded. I was too young to either know or translate these cuss words to English, but I understood she was asking me to not be a flamethrower when I grow up. These words were demonic fires—they burnt spirits and singed souls.

Mother's flat was in a Muslim mohalla, neighbourhood, next to a tyre gully. From Bandook Gully to Tyre Gully, both with a burning trail of smoke and fire. We had a new identity here. She got the flat through my father Khan Saab. He had introduced her to the builder as his wife, Rehana. She went along with it to get her foot in the door, but insisted on all the ownership paperwork in her Hindu name. She did not want to take a chance with him pretending to be her husband and usurping her property later. He was capable of it. If he was helping her own a place and settle in as a wedded couple, it meant she would allow him in her mujra despite his quirks, some of which included arriving drunk and foul-mouthed, singing along during her performance, trying to get intimate in a drunken state. Her new neighbours did not need to know the whole truth about her flat. The arrangement worked for her. She won over the neighbours with her charm and gifts, and told them the real story when the time was right.

During my winter vacations, my mother took me to various temples and mosques across Delhi, Rajasthan, Maharashtra and

Uttar Pradesh. That was her idea of how I should spend my holidays, or perhaps it was her own detox tour. She certainly seemed to enjoy the saadgi, simplicity, of spiritual cleansing at such venues. I did not care for these places. I found them loud, chaotic and messy, and at times was scared there would be a stampede, given the crowd. So much pushing and shoving, standing all night in a queue to get a glimpse of a marble deity, jostling for breathing space—God was a pain. Which is why reading the agent provocateur Nietzsche in my youth felt so revitalizing and relatable.

Mother gave food and money to the poor, distributed blankets, cooked deghs, cauldrons of biryani, and prayed for hours—weeping, sobbing, which only confused me. How could I have known she wished for a better life? She never told me her troubles. What would I have done knowing them? I saw her as a feisty, independent woman living on her own terms. I did not know she desired love, comfort and a life without adversity and hardship, which she made look effortless at the kotha.

She bought me an all-rides pass once at Appu Ghar in Delhi and sent me up alone on the giant wheel, the intimidating flying carousel, and the bumper cars. All I remember is being terrified and frozen, looking down at her from my seat in the giant wheel and waiting for the ordeal to end so I could return to her. She must have been watching my shocked face going up and down, round and round, and registering it as a smile because I was not screaming. Violence was long-pressing my mute button.

In Mathura, she swung on a Krishna jhoola on a tree—like the gopikas playing with Krishna. I clutched her sari, my head barely reaching her waist, my face nestled in her crotch as she flew into the skies. She was every bit a daredevil, and I a scaredy little mouse.

In Pushkar, we ate hot, juicy malpuas in a sweet shop inside a narrow lane close to the Brahma temple.

In Poona, we stayed at my grandmother Gullo's patre ka ghar, a tin hut with a cow tied to a khoonta, stake, outside. There were goats, chickens and ducks too. I had to choose between shitting in a field with grunting pigs around or on a railway track to avoid their interfering snouts. That, too, without tissue paper. It was a staple at the boarding schools, where water supply was limited. A smelly drain teeming with flies flowed outside the hut. There was nothing nice about being poor. Inside the hut, I watched the video of the song *Om Shanti Om* on a small black-and-white TV the size of a transistor radio. In the movie, Rishi Kapoor dances on a giant revolving LP disc under dazzling pink disco lights. He is wearing a shiny silver shirt and trousers, with the name of his character emblazoned on his back. Six background dancers accompany him on the disc, chorusing his la-la-las and gliding past the camera. Someone in the hut said my mother was one of the dancers. Really? I believed them. I inched closer to the TV and followed each dancer individually with my eyes, trying to spot her, my head spinning. *Woh gayi Mummy!* There she goes! I clapped as the disc revolved. The name of Rishi Kapoor's character is displayed in block lettering on stage: M O N T Y.

The same name as mine, with some variation: Montu, Mantu, Manto, depending on how the caller decides to tongue-twist my pet name for extra sweetness. I abhorred the variations, much less liked the name thereafter. My mother was in the audience during the filming of *Om Shanti Om*, where she worked as an extra. That is how she got the idea for my nickname. Rishi Kapoor was singing and dancing just like a tawaif, but in a modern space, a culture centre where he had legitimacy, where she fell in love with his talent and good looks, and thought Monty was a cool name. Bantoo, my grandmother Gullo called me. That variation I did not mind. She looked like a witch with a black dupatta covering her head. Dressed in a flowing black ghagra with a blouse that had cracked mirrors in it, she wore a thick silver hansli necklace around her tattooed neck. Green tattoo lines and dots on her chin and cheeks, nose ring, earring, armlet, anklet—I had not seen anyone like her. Her face was ravaged by seasons of silent grief. She smelt toasty. She sold desi daaru, local alcohol, and smoked a beedi. She walked with a hunch, supported by a wooden staff, making her look even more macabre. I once saw a studio photograph of her. It was a sepia tint image in which she looked older than the invention of photography. But she smiled when she spoke to me, her grey-brown eyes twinkling in shiny pools of opaque light. She took me to a milk shop to feed me the best lassi in Pimpri market. It was so thick and creamy that I had to eat it with a spoon.

In Bombay, we went to meet Mother's friends in Congress House, including Akku Aapa, a tawaif as old as history and full of engrossing tales around the fading tawaif culture. *Sab khatm ho gaya hai ab toh*, she said, limping around her room, offering sharbat and preparing a paan, cracking betel nut with a chunky silver sarota. *Topaz mein naach rahi hain aajkal.* Everything is over. These days the girls are dancing in Topaz Bar. She spat betel paint into an ugaldaan, a spittoon, with the precision of a sniper's aim. Not a single fleck of red fell on her starched white kurta.

Mother sat at the khadim's gaddi, the shrine attendant's seat, in the Ajmer dargah and joked, mingled and flirted back with the male pilgrims from Gujarat, but got along just as well with the women's side of the divided gaddi. Women who had travelled with their husbands from Pakistan or Dubai. Mother chose the middle spot, a bridge to both the sexes. An agile body, a friendly disposition and a lack of vanity made her popular with strangers everywhere. I watched her crack non-veg jokes, as they were called. One of the jokes was about two men inviting each other for a dinner feast. The rich man welcomes his poor friend to his shahi mahal, royal palace, and humbly calls it his gareeb khana, poorhouse, serving dishes bathed in riches whose fancy names the friend has never heard before. The poor friend invites the rich friend to his modest house, calling it a shahi mahal, and serves a greasy sweet rice dish called mootanjan, which the rich man enjoys, asking about the special fragrant ingredient in it. To which the poor friend comments, *Aur zyada accha hota, magar aaj moot thoda kam padh gaya.* It would have been better but I fell a little short of urine. Another joke was about a woman challenging a group of men that she could tell any man's size. She kept winning at it until a man stepped forward and said, Sure, but I can piss in yours, can you piss in mine? The pilgrims listening to my mother in that sacred space tittered. I played innocent, wincing like I did not get it, but I was shocked. The dark humour, the pious atmosphere we were in, the lusty eyes of those men—my mother knew how to get them hot and bothered. She became one of the boys. Whereas, with the women, she would drape her dupatta over her head and recite devotional verse along with them, projecting the saintly grace of one who had renounced all earthly desires. I dutifully sat by her side on the gaddi, mattress, listening to the qawwals sing *Kirpa Karo Maharaj* in praise of Khwaja Sahib. She handed me ten-rupee notes to place with adab, salute, on their baaja as nazrana, tip.

It was in Ajmer that I had a strange, mystical encounter. I was still a kid when we attended the Urs festival. Crowds dressed in white looked like a shroud that was moving towards the inner chamber of the dargah. I was feeling stuffy in the jostle. I prayed at the gate: Khwaja Baba, if you love me, please come to me and take me inside the chamber and kiss me on my forehead as a sign that you love me.

No sooner had I said it than a tall lady walked up to me and asked, *Andar jaana hai?* You want to go in?

Yes, I said.

Come with me.

She held my hand. I held my mother's hand. We walked through the crowd like we were strolling in a park. No sweat. After a round through the inner chamber, the lady brought us back to the same spot where she had met me. She held my head, kissed me and disappeared into the crowd. It was only then that I understood what had happened. I turned to my mother and said, I had just wished for this. She sounded pleased and said, *Tu toh Khwaja Baba ki daen hai.* You are a gift from Khwaja Baba. I was supposed to assume I had dropped out of the sky into her lap. I was special. I highly doubted it. A mother's pamper is poisonous. Later comprehended as *laad-pyaar ne bigad diya*. A spoilt brat.

We travelled in smelly trains from Delhi to Ajmer, sitting by the sulphurous toilet in the Urs season when pilgrims outnumbered seats. My mother would often not buy a ticket for me. *Bachcha hai,* he is a child, as she passed me off to ticket collectors. On occasions when the officer was not convinced and tried to fine her, she would walk away, saying, Keep the child. She had mastered the art of abandoning me at railway stations.

In Agra, we drank water from a well and ate malida in the house of the sarpanch, village chief, who had the only television in the village. The sarpanch was related to a tawaif in Calcutta who had taken us to her village. Oh, and malida! That distinct taste of ghee and jaggery mashed together with bajre ki roti has never left my tongue till date. It was my madeleine cake moment. The entire village sat on the floor of the sarpanch's courtyard, watching television in the evening, while I sat on a khaat, feeling royal, spooning delicious malida into my mouth. Mother showed me the Taj Mahal, but did not tell me what it stood for—just like the time her mother-in-law, who never explained its significance, took her to the Taj Mahal garden for a picnic lunch. Even more strange was that at the Agra station, where my mother had sent me to fetch tea from a stall, two strangers asked me what I was doing in Agra. I said I had come to see the Taj Mahal. They laughed and said they were locals who had not seen it. I found that very odd, considering how far we had travelled to see it. I did not tell my mother about the strangers. I suppose another child would recount it like a shaggy dog story. I was not that kid. I was the kid who preferred keeping strangeness to himself. Especially if it involved me chatting with beautiful, young men.

For instance, every year in Ajmer, we would visit the same stall to buy cane tashtaris, trays brimming with fragrant rose petals, and velvet chaadars as offerings for the tomb of Khwaja Moinuddin Chishti. The phoolwala, a striking young man in a Pathan suit and white skullcap, had a gaze that spoke volumes without a single word passing between us. He would place a skullcap on my head or tie a handkerchief with quiet familiarity. In his eyes, and in the glances of other men, I sensed a longing—or a recognition of something different in me. Their looks carried a silent vow, a promise to guard my unspoken truth. Their smiles were not mere kindness but a nod to a shared, secret code. My gaydar, like an antenna tuned to far-off galaxies, caught these covert signals—encrypted, tucked away in my mind to keep the world's chaos at bay.

In Kanpur, an old man shared our large bed in a hotel room. I know now that the old man was Shekhar, a patron my mother had met in her early years. She maintained he was one of the nicest gentlemen she had ever come across in her life. I did not see my mother get intimate with the old man, so I cannot be sure of the nature of their relationship—although, from what I have just mentioned above, my mother must have thought I was too young to retain this memory. It is not a violent memory, though.

Many years later, I saw Gullo before she died in Poona. I was a teenager then. She was sprawled on a jute mat on the floor of a dingy room in the chawls of Bhat Nagar, Pimpri. She smelt sour. The woman whose face I likened to an arid landscape that had weathered many a dusty storm, now had the haunted eyes of a parched mirage in search of its oasis. She asked me for something sweet, her memory no longer an aide in recognizing me. She gesticulated with her hand to her mouth and throat. She could not eat the thick lassi.

Who are you? she asked.

Dulari's son, I said.

Who Dulari?

Her daughter, whom she fondly called Dulari, the dear one.

Memory so volatile that it is quite possible some important bits slip away in the churning of recall.

I laughed and fetched a bottle of Coke for her. She had fetched me so many bottles of milk when I was an infant, oiling and massaging my tiny bones to strengthen them. She wanted to pierce my ears, tattoo my body like hers, but Mother prohibited her from using my body as a canvas for the Kanjarbhat tribe and its totems. Kothas are already sullied—why make it worse for a child from there?

Gullo drank from the Coke bottle like a hungry fawn sucking a doe's teat. That is my clearest memory of her. So violently tender.

# The Eighties

Growing up in the Bowbazar kotha, my mother did not speak a lot to me—instructing me to fetch her a daab, coconut, from the market, gaathiya, a deep-fried snack from a sweet shop, or ojhdi, a goat offal snack I found too repulsive to even taste, from the soodi khana, a local drinking den. Small talk was never part of her vocabulary with me. I was produced for grand statements. She had big plans. She forbade her patrons from asking me to fetch them a cigarette or gutka. Some kids did it for small change. My child is not here to run your errands, she scolded them. Everyone in the mohalla knew me before I could make their acquaintance. Some spoke curtly, some lasciviously, some indifferently. I did not want attention, but my demeanour attracted it. Shy and quiet, speaking only when addressed directly, not indulging in chit-chat and keeping my gaze down made it even more conspicuous that I was a tawaif's child. Or I was acting out my own tawaif tendencies. I was what I saw. And all it took to confirm was for any one of them to ask, *Kahaan rehte ho?* Where do you live? Bandook Gully, I would say softly, demurely. Oh, it elicited from a shopkeeper, followed by a forced smile. The silence after the 'oh' was incriminating. Maybe I was a sensitive child who felt accursed.

Once, when Mother asked me to fetch her a paan, the paanwala teased me, *Kab mila rahe ho apni mummy se?* When are you going to introduce me to your mother? It was the way he said it, leeringly, making his customers giggle, shaming me, making me wait longer than usual. I was in tears. I knew when a man was being vulgar. It was a common sight at the kotha. The women knew how to deal with such men. I went home crying and complained to my mother. She immediately walked out with me and scolded him. *Khabardar jo mere bachche se aisa ganda mazak kiya toh. Tu aa kothe pe, mujra karwati hoon tera!* Don't you dare use your dirty jokes on my child. You come to the kotha, I'll make you dance! He never dared to joke with me again. My mother was a trooper. But how many men could she shield me from? People stared, murmured when I stepped out alone. Maybe it was the way I walked. There was always instrumental music playing inside my head when I walked. Drums, pipes, strings. I choreographed each step like I was hopping on to giant water lily leaves strewn across a pond. Sometimes, a stray tune floating in from a radio on the street entered my body and took over. I turned and leapt, but it was done subtly—I danced like no one was watching. No one could tell. Unlike the choreomania, the very obvious dancing plague that broke out in Strasbourg in 1518, where people danced non-stop for days on end and died doing so. My style was discreet. I madly related to Sridevi's character Anju in *Chaalbaaz*, whose body slavishly reacted to Indian classical music. She could not control herself but dance at the drop of a beat. Was it a dancing disease? I wanted it. But I also did not want it to be so obvious. My moves were of a tawaif. Slow, sinuous, sensual. Moving was dancing.

Mother told me to read my books, which I found dull compared to her dances. The kotha is no place to study, really. It is nearly impossible to put a child to focus. May I digress here to quote William Faulkner, who once said that a brothel, somewhat similar to a kotha, is an ideal environment to write. He said:

> Art is not concerned with environment either; it doesn't care where it is. If you mean me, the best job that was ever offered to me was to become a landlord in a brothel. In my opinion it's the perfect milieu for an artist to work in. It gives him perfect economic freedom; he's free of fear and hunger; he has a roof over his head and nothing whatever to do except keep a few simple accounts and to go once every month and pay off the local police. The place is quiet during the morning hours, which is the best time of the day to work. There's enough social life in the evening, if he wishes to participate, to keep him from being bored; it gives him a certain standing in his society; he has nothing to do because the madam keeps the books; all the inmates of the house are females and would defer to him and call him 'sir'. All the bootleggers in the neighbourhood would call him 'sir'. And he could call the police by their first names. So the only environment the artist needs is whatever peace, whatever solitude, and whatever pleasure he can get at not too high a cost.

He may as well be talking about my living conditions, except that the child me would have to be sent to a boarding school for an education, develop a passion for writing, return to the kotha and put his theory to the test.

I stood outside Mother's room when she was performing, and studied her moves to imitate later, when she was not around. I put my hand under the almirah in the half-room, a cold, dark place where she snuck her brass ghungroos. It felt like putting my hand inside a snake's pit. I put my cheek to the floor, peeped in and tapped the tips of the shining, golden metal bells to the floor. They made a low chham-chham sound, just like in the movies, where a tawaif walked gracefully, haltingly, into a mehfil to perform her mujra. I could spend hours lying there, tapping the ghungroos. Imagination is a child's deepest secret. Perhaps connecting it to the movies fascinated me more than seeing my mother or the other women in the kotha wear it every evening. It was a common sight, like they were wearing their work shoes. They did not wear it and sashay around all day. That would have been so unmusical—a jarring melange of chunky sounds. They wore it in the afternoon if an ustadji turned up for kathak practice. They wore it in the middle of a performance when they were singing and decided to dance. They usually wore it in front of the patron. Wearing it so must have been part of the act—the patrons enjoyed watching the tawaif draw out her red, hennaed feet and bind them in a torture device, a bondage strap. The tawaif pulled on the ghungroo strings and tightened them strongly to stimulate the patron's kinks. The patrons felt their throats parch with lust. They reached for their whisky glasses.

The ghungroos were heavy to the touch. Dragging them out from under the almirah would disturb their sleep. They were resting there, like a coiled snake. Stacked one on top of the other, they resembled a guchchaa, a bundle of metallic flower buds about to burst open, and within each bud a small, round pellet swam like a pearl inside an oyster. Sometimes, these metal balls fell out. I collected them to make my own pair of ghungroos. Meanwhile, I fashioned myself some dizzyingly high heels from Pan Parag and Baba Zarda dabbas, tin boxes. I tied them with canvas shoelaces to my feet and walked like a circus performer on stilts. I sang *Bijlee girane main hoon aayi/Kehte hain mujhko hawa hawaai.* Since I was strictly ordered to not touch my mother's shoes and ghungroos, and I was mostly obedient, I sought inventive ways to exercise my desires. Mother did not spend any money on toys, so what else was I supposed to do? A boy obsessed with Sridevi is another strong indicator that this child is more than just a little bit queer. I duplicated her dance moves in *Himmatwala*, *Nagina*, *Tohfa*, *Masterji*, *Mawaali*, *Nazrana*, *Ram Avtar*, *Mr India* and *Guru* in those fake tin heels. I wobbled like Sridevi in *Na Jaane Kahan Se Aayi Hai* from *Chaalbaaz*, putting extra zing into my steps and toppling melodramatically on the line *Kisi ke haath na aayegi yeh ladki*. I thought of Sridevi as my on-screen mother—a superb dancer training me in Mother's absence. Incidentally, if you are a trivia collector, this song features a poster of the film *Raiszaada*, which loosely means a rich brat, a term used to describe a spoilt patron at the kotha. Govinda, apart from being a nimble dancer, plays the titular character in the film. His mother, Nirmala Devi, going by rumours at the kotha, belonged to a tawaif family from Banaras. She had previously done some acting and playback. She sang a bhajan, *Jai Ambe, Jai Jagdambe*, her only playback, in her son's film *Raiszaada*. Govinda is reticent about his mother's background. In case you are wondering what the connection is to my story, God is in the details if you connect the dots using the trivia as clue.

At the Darjeeling boarding school Daffodils, my mother was late for my admission. She tried to humour the principal, saying, *Yeh padhai mein bahut accha hai. Ek class toh jump bhi kar gaya Kurseong mein.* He is a good student. He even advanced to a higher grade in Kurseong. She laughed, convincing the principal. He was a burly man, who I later found out was nicknamed Bulldog by senior students, but not for his hangdog expression. He did not have one. He wore a brown suit, had slick hair, was clean-shaven and had red eyes. He was kind enough to not make me sit for an admission test. He looked at me, asked a few questions—my name, interests—and found me to be bright. *Thoda sa shy hai,* my mother said. He is a little shy. Nervousness made her speak more than required.

Where is his father? The principal asked her.

*Woh neeche khade hain*, she said. He is standing downhill.

Why?

Knee problem, she lied.

There was no father standing downhill at the Jeep taxi stand. In fact, when the principal asked for my father's name on the admission form, she lied again. This one was a repeat lie. I was a repository of her secrets and lies. Previously, at the Kurseong boarding school, she had named her elder sister Babbo's husband, Anoop Gagade, as my father, when the principal of that school was reluctant to put her name down as the sole guardian.

Anoop Gagade, she said.

Anoop what? the principal asked.

Gagade, she mumbled.

Gaikwad? he asked. Gaikwad? he repeated, seeking her assurance.

*Haan, wahi,* she said. Yes, that one. She nodded and went along with it. A few years later, I began spelling Gaikwad with an 'e' to match the spelling of Shivaji Rao Gaekwad, or Rajinikanth, as we know him.

Aye Gaikwad, are you related to Anshuman? Students and teachers teased me. Gaikwad was an unusual surname in the hills. I was tired of being related to the cricketer. I did not play cricket. I preferred watching films, a better use of my playtime. No, I said, I am closer to Shivaji Rao Gaekwad. Who is that? It perplexed many. Revealing his screen name also revealed my interest in general knowledge, impressing some and distancing many others for my know-it-all disposition. Another name I felt a kinship with was Parvati Khan, the singer. She had sung *Jimmy Jimmy Jimmy, Aaja Aaja Aaja* in *Disco Dancer*. It was a big hit. I had seen her perform on the DD National television channel and was quite intrigued by her name. Parvati, for the Hindu deity of power; Khan for, well, being Muslim, while also being Hindu. It was a fantastic idea that one could be both, not convert. I secretly harboured a desire to call myself Manish Khan. I wanted to be of both faiths. My father, Khan Saab, had shown no mercy in giving me his name, and so I was stuck with a fictional surname.

I walked up a flight of stairs, opened the door, blocking the light at the entrance and bashfully asked in my thin, singsong voice, Is this Class 3? Much, much later in life, a school friend recalled that moment, saying I stood there like a prophetic child-figure in that foggy light and my long coat. I thought you were a girl, she said. Long coat? I said. Probably your memory is dramatic, but it suits my entry.

Boy confused for a girl. Mother had certainly not raised me like a boy. She did not raise me like a girl either. There was no gender norm routine in the kotha. So if someone's first impression of me was that I was a girl, I did not fight it. So be it. If they were shocked to find out later that I was a boy, it was not my mistake that they were previously confused, right? I simply did not bother to correct them.

I was the principal's favourite child in my first year. Some kid complained that their precious pen was stolen. Boarders were gathered in the dining hall in the evening. The principal was urging us to own up, when suddenly he pulled me out of the crowd. He turned me around to face the students. This is the face of innocence, he said. I know this boy did not steal the pen. Blood rushed to my cheeks. I could get away with murder. He was using me as a pawn to make a chess move. I had not stolen the pen. Whoever has stolen the pen, he said, come out. No one did.

In defence of my innocence in those days, I saw two dogs stuck at the rear, running to and fro near the dining hall. What happened to them, I asked a girl. Someone glued them, she said. We felt sorry for the distressed dogs, watching them jump. I pray for their separation, I said. They must be in so much pain. The same, excruciating pain I felt watching a pig being impaled in a back alley by the school's wood stockpile. A spear was pierced through its squealing heart. Later that evening, the meat was served in a delicious broth with sel-roti, a Diwali special dinner. At the time, I did not connect the killing to the feast. I ate heartily, thinking I was served chicken and assuming the school knew I was not supposed to consume pork. Mother had conspiratorially whispered into my ear, *Suar ka gosht kabhi mat khaana, haan, haraam hai.* Don't eat pig meat, it's forbidden. She was preserving the Muslim faith in my bloodstream from gustatory impurity. I only found out the truth after the meal was digested and the taste had soured into guilt. I approached a teacher. I told her that I should not have eaten it. It is paap, I said. I had not yet chanced upon the word 'sin'. She told me something so practical, it carved itself into my memory: When you meet God, he won't ask you what you ate—he will ask what good deed you did. In that moment, I understood—God did not follow religion the way humans did. I never confessed to Mother. That was my good deed. Religious beliefs could not dictate my diet. I sensed that the school was not a sanctuary—it was going to be a devil ride.

No one in school asked me where I came from, who my father was, what my mother did. Criminal to ask even, I guess, at that age, had I blurted the truth innocently. Kids were busy from five in the morning, when we woke up to the Kanchenjunga dew in our hair. We lined up to brush and wash, queued up for the toilet, completed homework before breakfast—two slices of stingily buttered bread, a boiled egg and sugarless, watery milk—got dressed for school, attended classes with day scholars, had lunch break, got watery tea and bread with some playtime at sunset, then back to the study table, dinner of rice, dal and a local produce called iskus, squash, or potatoes, and lights out by nine, in bed. We were really the chattel.

There were so many of us, who had time for small talk? And where could we find a quiet corner? It was a tiny school sitting atop a hill overlooking the magnificent and third-highest mountain in the world, run by an ex-army man, meaning strict rules. Children were huddled together like sheep, with no breathing space. Boarders got some leisure time on the weekends, when one could play all day. That was when someone lying on the cool grass, staring at the fat clouds animate into comic shapes, could have asked me questions about my background, as could I have asked them. But none of this happened like films will have you believe—cute young kids bonding. And because I did not spend time with the boys, a lot of my time was spent in my own quiet company.

Girls were my closest allies at the hostel. I followed them like their sacrificial lamb. It must have been the most natural thing for me to do because the kotha was all female too. I sang and said I could dance along to entertain them. I wanted to be part of their gang. Where did you learn to dance, a senior monitoring the girls asked. By watching my mother. She is a dancer, I said. Where does she dance? On stage, I said nonchalantly, proudly. I was not entirely lying. Mother did perform in stage shows across cities. Show us, they said. This was my chance! I twirled like a bee drunk on nectar. I showed them the gol chakkar, spinning to form a circle. I showed them Sridevi's knee-dance in *Main Teri Dushman*. I did the Nagin dance, the Nataraj tandav and even Mithun's disco moves. Needless to say, I aced the audition. A radio played in a house downhill. I picked up the lyrics instantly. Songs such as *Aye Mere Humsafar Ek Zara Intezar*, *Keh Do Ke Tum* or *Har Kisi Ko Nahi Milta*. The girls were impressed at how fast I learnt the words and could teach them. They put me in a dress, tied ghungroos to my feet and made me perform on stage on Founder's Day. The song was *Jhoom Jhoom Nache Mayuri*. I was well aware of the melody. I suggested it. It was one of those songs, and the film, in fact, *Nache Mayuri*, that was so inspiring to me as a child. The film showed Sudha Chandran, dancer-actress depicting her real life story of pursuing her passion for dance after she lost a leg in a road accident. She was my hero. If she could do it, why could I, an able-bodied kid from a kotha, not? And I was going to wear ghungroos on stage. Just like my mother! There was one problem, though. At the kotha, whenever I danced on the tawaifs' demand, I was a kid entertaining them by imitating the sensual moves of my mother or of her friend Meena, who was dark, squat, curvy—way more sexy without even trying. The tawaifs did not dress me up. They did not put ghungroos on my feet. They laughed and applauded my efforts, saying, *Bilkul apni mummy ke jaise apna kulha chalata hai.* That I swayed my hips exactly like my mother. If one of them teased me as nachkaiyaa launda, a derogatory word for a boy who danced, it bristled me, flushing my cheeks red with embarrassment, but it did not linger. Loosely put, I was everyone's favourite nautch boy in my mother's absence. *Bachcha hi toh hai.*

But it was a different story at the boarding school. I was thrust on stage and asked to show it to the world outside. Would I succeed? Fail? Run away? My classmates were confused to see me in a yellow frock and dupatta, wearing ghungroos, jewellery and red lipstick. The older girls at the hostel had dressed me up for fun. It startled everyone when my name was announced as the next performer. As the music played and I danced, *Jhoom jhoom jhoom jhoom nach mayuri*, I forgot my steps, stumbled, regained my posture, twirled, looked at the audience as a distinct blur—unrecognizable in silence. Was it horrified or was it just my fuzzy reading of the room? *Chhann chhana nana nan nach mayuri.* I had to stomp my ghungrooed feet in a moving-forward step like a peacock strutting in vanity. Instead, I dragged my feet backwards, like a peahen getting away from my flashy steps. I do not recall exactly what I did. One thing was certain—I was successfully alienating myself from the crowd. Boys stopped interacting with me, singling me out like I was diseased with a dancing disorder. The principal asked me to play football with the kids. I stood at one end of the field, in my white shorts, not moving.

What are you doing? the principal asked.

What to do, sir, I said, the ball is only not coming to me. I was that kind of a prophet, I guess. I could have danced my way to the ball, but were the boys who despised me not already dancing around it? Is the game of football also not a form of dance? Why should I interrupt their ball dance? The principal slapped his forehead and gave up. How was he going to raise a queer boy here? He made it worse when he said the shattering glass is made of sugar and the sludgy mud of chocolate. He was describing to me a violent action scene in a film where two men exchanged blows. I had shut my eyes. I really believed the principal. He was putting the magic back into the movies—a primal source of imagination for a queer boy, where anything was possible. Except me taking an active interest in kicking a ball, as if I would hurt it.

One night, I woke up with a funny stomach. I knocked on the principal's bedroom and asked to use his toilet. The toilet for the boys was too far away, downstairs, by which time I would have shit my pants. He gave me a shot of brandy and put me to sleep on the couch. I woke up fine the next morning, thinking of the time I saw a patron make a tawaif's kid sip from his whisky glass during her performance. The little boy danced like a jamura for his madari, a monkey for his master. Everyone laughed, including the tawaif. I was shocked then, but now, after having tasted alcohol as medicine, a magic potion, rather, I had to re-evaluate that memory.

That little monkey boy Bunny was older than me. Once, at the kotha, he was caught kissing me when I was five or six. I was lying under his weight in an empty room that belonged to a tawaif, who was probably out shopping. He was sitting on my stomach. Another tawaif spotted us and reported us to our mothers. His mother beat him. I did not understand why. What horrible thing had he done? He must have seen someone do it, maybe in a movie? His kisses were not violent. My mother beat me as well. I did not understand why I, too, was being whacked. I could not have possibly seduced him at my age. Thereafter, when the boys played hide-and-seek in the afternoon, Bunny and I hid behind a curtain and kissed. It felt great when another boy fondled me. This was an early indicator of my orientation. Those who opposed it, our mothers, were violent with us. But when we found an intimate space, it felt good. So we did it even more frequently, perhaps as a form of resistance against those who punished us for it. Did that make us children masochists? I was experiencing and expressing my sexuality quite early. Playing with the girls also involved some perfunctory kissing in the kitchen-set game or the doctor-doctor game, where we would touch our private parts and giggle, but that did not thrill me so much as what was forbidden and done secretly with the boys behind curtains and under quilts in pin-drop silence—as if this was illegal to engage in publicly.

In the beginning, my sexual experiments must have been a reaction to the violence. I did not seek it, but when a boy initiated it, I did not deny its sensual pleasures. It was around this time that the secret games of the kotha slipped into my quilt in the hostel and continued to be a pleasurable game to me. A handsome boy my age, Vaibhav, who played football, sneaked into my lower bunk bed from his bed across. He told me a story about a romantic couple. Most likely his parents. A fairy tale, he said. Do you know how they kissed? he asked. How would I? This part was not in the Hans Christian Andersen books. No, I said. He re-enacted it with me. He then pulled my pyjamas down. What are you doing? I asked. Sssh, he said, I am showing you how they loved each other. We rubbed our bodies together. It was exciting and dangerous. What if a matron walked by and caught us? We had to be absolutely silent, like the stars winking at us. We became night-time lovers like the moon and the clouds outside the tall French windows in the dormitory, giving us both light and shade, hide-and-seek. He said we could play husband and wife. I was going to be the wife—but naturally, I had the shy and quiet demeanour for it. I was the girlier boy of the two—he, of course, although in my eyes fair and pretty, was a stud on the football field. Clichéd times, I suppose, the uninformed '80s. I did not mind the role play. I was all set for pregnancy through a kiss. A senior student caught us snogging on a weekend afternoon in bed. He did not complain to the teachers. Instead, he asked me to meet him behind the canteen. He tried to kiss me. I resisted. I will tell everyone, he said. I ran away and informed my studly husband. Vaibhav challenged the senior boy, saying he would inform the teachers that the senior was harassing the two of us. The senior backed out. Vaibhav had some solid conviction there. Sadly, he stopped sneaking into my bed at night. The marriage was short-lived.

Young boys my age who were fondling me at the kotha and now at the hostel … what must have been on their minds? Did they see me as a girl? A substitute for a girl? I was not making cow eyes at them. I did not have sexual thoughts. How did it start? My equal and consensual participation in these acts of passion … where did that stem from? I did not know right from wrong. I responded to and embraced their touch. However, I never initiated it. I never took the first step. Does that mean I was enacting the passive role of the traditional girl, who only responds to the advances of a boy? And what about the fact that it was towards any and every boy who approached me softly, gently, lovingly? When the senior boy demanded it, I refused.

At the kotha, Chaman, the wastrel adult brother of the skinny Meena Bai, had begun ambushing me in the dark gully and forcibly kissing me. His spiky beard dug like porcupine needles into my cheeks, turning them pink. That I did not like. He was rough. I complained to my mother. She told him to stop troubling me. He laughed and said he was teasing me. He did not stop. I dreaded stepping out. The young boys who played cricket in the gully in the afternoon began teasing me. Some called me a chhakka, a derogatory term for a trans or intersex person; some called me naazuk, another taunt for a feminine boy; some called me a girl; and some called me a randi ka beta, son of a whore. What had I done to provoke them? In these narrow lanes, where the courtesans of Calcutta thrived, and where a messiah had not reached to protect them, the words boomeranged in the air, as if someone had announced the title of a new grindhouse thriller: *Shaitaan Ka Beta*, *Jungle Ka Beta*, *Aladdin Ka Beta*, *Randi Ka Beta*. I was never pleased about the radio broadcast. I walked as far away from the din as I could, scraping my shoulder against the wall of a house to avoid inviting violence. The hubbub of insults would die out soon when the boys grew up, or if I had the temerity to approach them and cup their fuming crotch. In which case, I would not be alive to be writing this. Verbal abuse made me unflappable—the more they laughed, the more resilient I became. It is not bravery—just a kind of surrender that is equal parts cowardice and fait accompli triggered by being branded a randi ka beta, I suppose.

The kotha was a dilapidated fort that protected me from the prying eyes of patrons who could have been potential predators. The same prying eyes that bore through the women's artifice of sequinned blouses and scented gajras could not find a trace of me when they entered the courtyard. We were tucked away when the mujras began. Porous musical notes floated out to the streets in the evening, stirring the hearts and loins of louche men. Roadside ruffians who mocked me wished that I would lead them to the mujra dens as their sycophant pimp. They used to beckon me with sharp whistles and hoots when their wallet and groin were tumescent with their desire for a randi ka beta as a substitute for the real thing. An effeminate pimp's waggish manners might have suited me, but it was a job I never applied for, despite my unimpeachable qualifications in their eyes as a randi ka beta. Women, young girls and me—it seemed we were the only targets. A tawaif's brother, or an older child, was never seen inside the kotha. They preferred to hang out with the street rowdies instead of with the womenfolk at home. The boys were not training to be pimps, but to be men of honour. They were trying to groom their own macho identities away from the illicit world of their fussy mothers and sisters. Their worthless lives had no place in the contentious society outside the crumbling walls of the kotha, where they were welcomed as a randi ka beta.

The kotha boys were fighting the young men who catcalled them as randi ka beta. These kids were getting bashed, punching back, bleeding from wounds and courting the lacklustre law-and-order situation in the area. Policemen would referee fights, arrest scoundrels and demand bribes. The kotha boys soon began visiting sex workers in Sonagachi or the other kothas in the vicinity—Satta Wandi, Ramkali Ki Baari, Kallu Ki Baari, Sardar Ki Baari, places I sometimes visited with my mother when she took me along to meet her tawaif friends. The older boys consumed alcohol, smoked, did drugs and came home to quarrel with their mothers and sisters. They detested their environment, but did not know how to break free from the indignity of being a randi ka beta. All that I saw and heard and felt was unmitigated violence in the suffocating air.

The next year on Founder's Day in school, I danced to *Sun Sahiba Sun*. This time I twirled so hard for audience approval that I fell backstage. As the playback singer Lata Mangeshkar sang the line, *Ho, maine tujhe chunn liya, tu bhi mujhe chunn*, the chorus followed with the refrain *Chunn, chunn*. I bounced back on stage and continued with *Chunn, chunn*. I was choosing the audience. The audience was not sure what to make of me. Was I a boy wanting to be a girl? No one laughed. There were no claps either.

An English teacher named Suzanna had warned me backstage before my performance. Boys don't do these things, she had said in a sharp disciplinarian tone. That must have shaken my confidence. I did not have the time to react as she announced my name to perform. She was a teacher I idolized for her larger-than-life persona. She was always so immaculately dressed in bright pink and yellow minis, wore polished patent leather high heels, chunky gold jewellery, had the reddest lipstick possible that would contrast with skin as fair as hers, and matched with a perfectly coiffured bouffant—really a modern English version of a tawaif, if there was such a thing. She even had a gold tooth to blind us when she was in a charitable mood to smile on one of us poor earthlings. Her dazzling style was a fashion benchmark in a school where the rest of the drab teaching staff could be put in one corner, and she in another, and she would outshine all of them just by her radiant appearance alone. In fact, she taught us the word 'macho'. I did not use it because the pronunciation just fell a letter short of saying 'machod'. Dangerously close to motherfuck. So, in a way, she was telling me I was not macho enough to be a man? I was just a boy! She was embarrassed of me. What worse fate could I have summoned? Surely, I would have to stop acting like a girl. I was not dancing because I wanted to be a girl. I was not into dress-up and make-up. It was easily accessible to me at the kotha. I never put it on. Okay, once, the tawaifs did my make-up, put me in Gudiya's frock and made me dance to *Mere Haathon Mein Nau Nau Choodiyaan Hain*—just once, when my mother was out. She walked in on our little game. She did not reprimand us. But we stopped playing immediately. I got out of the frock, rubbed the red lipstick off and forgot all about it. I played with her chiffon dupattas only when

I was performing a role for the tawaifs or for a boy playing the hero. I never harboured a desire to wear her sari, blouse, chuttiya, bindi (plenty of which dotted the mirror like twinkling stars) or any of her jewellery. What the schoolgirls were doing to me was no different than what the tawaifs did. I was only enacting what I knew best. If I was raised in another environment, perhaps I would be fixing a broken cycle on stage, no? Would that be fun to watch?

The boys at the hostel began teasing me, calling me a girl, chhakka and sissy. I did not fight back. The English teacher's comment stayed with me. If I was not supposed to sing and dance in a costume, what else was I supposed to do? I took shelter in the library—a safe place to distract my thoughts and allow immense possibilities. I spent time reading comics, *Winnie the Pooh* being one of the first that I picked, magazines *Sputnik* and *Misha*, writing essays, designing my own greeting cards with cut-outs of cartoon characters from old *Archies* comics, after reading and stealing them from the library to gift to my girlfriends, many of whom were my rakhi sisters—it was quite a fad to have a rakhi brother in the interest of receiving a packet of coconut sweets from the mooh-bola, sworn, brother. I did not have the money for sweets, so the cards flew off the library racks.

If I were to stop dancing, could I write, produce and direct a play in the coming year? I was standing on my toes, stretching my arms up for the least-read dusty titles stacked on the highest shelf in the library. It was a great exercise to nurture such a towering ambition. Nothing was beyond reach if curiosity stoked the mind. I recalled watching a play in my previous school in Kurseong. It was about a master who instructs his servant to treat a guest well after he leaves home for work. The silly servant confuses a tramp for the arriving guest and mistreats the expected guest, who arrives later. I staged it on the next Founder's Day. I did not take up an acting part. I was the stage director. I mean, I did not know the term back then, but it felt good for a change, to not be the main source of ridicule on stage. My dancing skills were clearly not cutting with this tough crowd.

I could not tell if my recreation of the play was a success. We heard a few claps, maybe to cue us off stage. The actor playing the tramp wolfed down a packet of coconut biscuits in his performance, when I had clearly instructed him to leave a few for some of us backstage. The biscuit was our budget. Those who performed on Founder's Day got a treat in the canteen—a plate of aloo-dum puri, or momo and tea. This was one of the primary reasons for me to bandy a bunch of amateur actors together and stage a play. Greed motivated us. In my two previous efforts as a dancer, I went to the canteen, sat in a corner and ate my free meal, still smudged with half-washed lipstick and eyeliner, alone—not quite happy, not entirely sad.

My mother asked the principal to celebrate my birthday with a cake. She had paid extra fees in advance. She had earlier packed in a cream-coloured Rajiv Gandhi safari suit in my school trunk. *Tres chic*. I was told to ditch my dull-grey sweater and navy blue shorts, our school uniform. I stood out at the morning assembly as the only odd white patch in a sea of grey and blue. A glitch. I distributed sweets to my classmates. It felt like I was a politician campaigning for acceptance while showing off these perks I enjoyed. It had never been done before in the school's running history. A student dressed in his birthday suit. Not the one you are now imagining. A photographer was called. I posed with my friends. At tea time, when the boarders changed into their hostel uniform, I kept my suit on, greeting them in the dining room with sweets or cake, depending on whom I favoured. Everyone wanted to be my friend for that sweet, heavenly slice of chocolate cake. Even if just for a day. I was a regal prince without an empire. It was the cleverest thing my mother had done so far. Her absence was not missed from the celebration. It seemed like she was the Queen Mother, who made a trunk call in the evening to check if everything had gone as smoothly as she had planned.

The school's only telephone was in the principal's bedroom through a flight of squeaky wooden stairs. We were instructed to walk up slowly, carefully, not to make a noise. The principal's wife shouted from her window: Trunk call for Manish! Come up in five minutes. I ran up and stood at the top of the stairs, not entering the bedroom until permitted. In my excitement, I had forgotten the climbing rule—walk slowly. The phone rang. Oh, it surely rang a deafening gong in my thumping, pacing heart!

Hello, my mother checked in her inquisitive tone.

Hello, I followed her softly.

I used to be the child attached to her sari's aanchal, never leaving it, hiding in its gauzy folds. It was my purdah from an unsafe world outside. Hearing her on the phone, so far away, coming close like this was fraught with mixed emotions. My eyes welled up. Our first phone conversation.

Happy birthday, Montu beta, Mother said in her gentlest, smiling voice.

I could see her crooked front teeth gleaming through the phone's receiver, her nose crinkling, her eyes going soft.

But for that terrible pet name I was instantly teleported back.

My voice choked, mixed with gratitude and longing. I whispered, Thank you.

*Zor se bol. Kya hua?* she asked. Speak louder. What happened?

How could I tell her our strict madam was in the room?

Thank you, I said, raising my pitch, clearing my throat.

We spoke briefly. My eyes brimmed with joyful tears, nearly blinding my vision. Trunk calls were expensive. My mother did not own a phone. She must have used Meena Aunty's.

Thank you, Ma'am, I said to our madam on my way out, grinning with discipline and impeccable manners. She nodded approvingly, looking busy reading *Stardust* film magazine, which would have been the perfect birthday gift for me.

The school had strange rules. Weekly tests were conducted on a subject. The top three students were announced, who shook hands with the principal in the morning assembly. Names of children who had failed were called out. They had to go and stand in a corner. After the assembly was dispersed following students singing *Jana Gana Mana*, the failed students were caned. Either the principal, or a PT teacher, brought down a thin, swift and swinging cane on the students' calves. Whoosh, whoosh, whoosh … three painful strikes. Exercise for the caning teacher or sadomasochist pleasure, who knows? Students who had passed the weekly test marched in line out of the field towards their classrooms, watching the punishment in silence and horror. The failed students immediately ran towards their class, their calves swollen red with the cane's long welt imprints. This form of punishment had another adverse effect on the boarders. The day scholars who were punished went home and had a parent apply ointment to their bruises. But there was no first aid kit for the boarders. Our outing was cancelled. Double punishment. This was harsh, cruel and really stung the heart, and made one miserable watching the other kids step out in joy with excitedly polished shiny shoes and neatly combed blazers. They patted their hair in a window's reflection in the absence of a mirror in the dorm, and looked like they were marching to receive a bravery award.

Once a month, the boarders were given outing money, or pocket money in the range of twenty to fifty rupees, according to their seniority in class, to go treat themselves at the market. Enjoy and behave yourself, said the madam doling out the cash, sternly instructing us. Mall Road was a five-kilometre uneven trek, dodging barking dogs that chased us on the uphill paths, or a five-rupee journey from Dali, a steep walk downhill, where the Jeeps plied.

Boarders spent the day in town eating momos or samosa-jalebi, buying greeting cards from Das Studio, spending extravagantly on ice cream, or on a chocolate shake and a hot dog at Keventer's. Buying biscuits, sweets and cake was our main agenda. Glenary's, though, was still too posh, too unaffordable for boarders. One looked at its richly painted creamy windows the colour of their popular cream rolls and went elsewhere to pick an ersatz. As it is, boarders did not have access to the school canteen like the day scholar kids, who had home-made tiffin plus snack money. Window shopping was a luxury for us. The boarders could go to the canteen after school only if their parents submitted advance canteen fees. Juniors were allowed five rupees a day, seniors could get ten or twenty rupees, depending on how much pocket money their guardians allowed. No money was given in hand.

The canteen owner, Yangdoma, an old lady with a crooked leg and a limp with its own two-beat rhythm in a clog, scribbled names and dues in a logbook. She collected cash at the end of the month from the principal's office. The legend was that she had survived a landslide that had nearly buried her and twisted her leg. No man wanted to marry her thereafter. A bitch, Kanchi, hobbled by her side. Yangdoma had a loud voice and a beautiful heart. She overlooked children stealing milk candy from her jar. A packet of Wai-Wai, churpi, battarey, sticky toffee, coconut biscuit, coconut sweet, aloo dum, momo, egg bun, tea with real milk or actual sugar—these were just some of the canteen snacks we dreamt of all day in our class, awaiting the final bell to be rung so that we could quickly make a dash to the canteen before it shut at sunset.

Boarders mainly relied on their school lunch, which was, at times, wholly unpalatable. A student took his plate back to the madam who served. Ma'am, he said, there is a worm in the rice. He had excavated a tiny wriggler from the grains at one end of his steel plate—an archaeological proof of our evolution. What to do then, she said, throw it and eat the rest. Some of us choked on a single grain in our mouth. Day scholars took pity on us and shared their tiffin. We craved their sandwich and fried rice. We got aloo, dal and rice. Senior boarders protested on the ground by arranging stones to spell 'No Aloo'. We were punished with squash and pumpkin for months. Food quality was consistently bad, but one learnt to swallow it without resentment when the stomach growled in hunger. The worm was chucked out with a ninja flick of the fork.

I did not fail in the weekly tests until I reached Class 5. Mathematics, and later Hindi, ruined my life. I spent my outing money on comics, cards, stickers and film magazines such as *Filmfare*, *Movie*, *Star & Style*, *Showtime*, *Stardust*, *Cine Blitz*—not all at the same time. I would sometimes get a samosa and a jalebi, or a scoop of vanilla ice cream. A kid caught stealing from a store was shaken by his collar and asked his name. He panicked and blurted out my name. The storeowner telephoned the principal to punish me. Luckily, the kid's accompanying friend informed the principal before I could be caned. Stealing was rampant in the hostel. Students arriving at the start of the year carried pickles, jams, butter, margarine, ghee, biscuit, namkeen, Horlicks, Bournvita, Maltova, Complan. It was locked and stored in a fat trunk called the tucks box, which stood at one end of the dining hall. The box was heavily dented on one side. A slim, thieving hand could slide in with some technical manoeuvring and steal a packet of biscuits or anything small that came within grasp. This operation worked like a claw machine in an amusement arcade. Only a few skilled and daring cat burglars could attempt it. Their identity was never known. Every morning at breakfast, or lunch, kids could pick out jars with their names labelled and choose to share with their friends at the table. Friendship status could be gauged by the rotation of a pickle jar if it did not reach a student. Students hid dry snacks in their clothes trunk, kept in a separate storeroom. Snacks hidden under their pillow, or in their cupboard and school bag, disappeared like a drug sniffed out by a K-9. Yet again, no thief was ever caught. Food simply disappeared like magic into a robber's alimentary canal without so much as a hiccup on its way down at high speed.

When the younger kids reached Class 5, they were moved to the all-boys' hostel from the current co-ed rooms next to the principal's bedroom. The boys' hostel was in a different house a hundred metres away from the school compound. There were four rooms with no doors between them from the main entrance. Class 5 and 6 students shared one room, those from Class 7 and 8 shared another, and so on. This way, the older boys from Class 9 and 10 did not intermingle with the younger boys. There was less chance of bullying in the dorm. A teacher lived in an adjacent room with her husband and two young sons. They kept a strict watch on the boys.

A boy from Bihar, Sujit, was admitted that year. He was in the same class as me, but slightly older than me and bigger in build. He began sneaking into my bed at night. Our beds were next to each other. I do not recall how it started. There was no fairy tale this time like Vaibhav. Sujit was quiet and passionate. We rarely spoke during school hours. We had nothing in common. It helped in keeping our night-time activity as clandestine as possible. In the dorm, he told us that in his village in Purnea, some people used to come to his house and gift his family a balloon that one could blow up with one's penis. He used a vernacular word for penis: Ling. *Sachchi,* he said, *mooh se nahi, neeche se phugaate hain.* He pointed at his crotch and enacted wearing an imaginary balloon on his penis. None of us had heard the L word before. Sure, I had heard lund and lowda in the kotha, but what was this chaste, musical word ling? He spoke a whole bunch of Hindi that most of us had trouble following. Our school did not permit speaking in any other language at all hours other than our first language, English. If someone snitched and reported us speaking in Hindi or Nepali, we were caned. Sujit did not care about the beating. He told us wondrous tales about cows and crows in his village. He had a word for the balloon: Nirodh. It was the first time many of us heard that word. Nirodh? What a quaint word, I thought. Sounds violent. How could one blow a balloon with one's penis? It was a wild joke, but one that stupefied me. *Sir, Nirodh ka kya matlab hota hai?* I asked our Hindi teacher. What does Nirodh mean? He was in a jocular mood. He loved rhymes. *Nirodh?* he said, sounding surprised. *Nirodh, jaise krodh, anger . . . jis se aap ko chahiye suraksha, ek suraksha kavach, yaani protection.*

A protection balloon? He did not say more. It did not add up. This was the same teacher who had previously told us dogala was when two necks embraced, explaining by breaking up the word in two parts—two for do and neck for gala. It elicited laughter. Now, I knew from the kotha that dogala was not an affectionate embrace. It was a slur about a person's hypocrisy. So there was ample reason to suspect the Hindi teacher was romanticizing these words to avoid addressing the question truthfully. Was it even correct to inform us about condoms? We had not seen a condom or even heard of it, or we could have done the maths ourselves. However, it was not long before I read about condoms, predictably in a Harold Robbins novel. When in doubt, find a library. That is where I had my orgasm-level epiphanies. I could now connect the ling to penis and the Nirodh to condom.

Around this time, I saw the film *Anubhav* at the kotha. It had been made a few years ago. In the film, a mischievous kid and his elder sister steal a packet of condoms belonging to the hero, who has come to the village to marry the sister. The brother-sister duo mistake the condoms for balloons, blow them up and tie them to a tree outside the hero's hut. The hero grabs the kid and blurts out: Nirodh. So you are the one who stole my Nirodh, my balloons?

He twists the child's ears. That is when I saw a visual of the famous Nirodh—a penis-protection balloon. Sujit was right. Interestingly, if you Google Nirodh's history, Wikipedia says that in 1963, when India manufactured its first mass-distribution condom, it was called Kamaraj, another name for Kamadeva, the Hindu deity of erotic love. Kamaraj was also the name of the then president of the ruling party, the Indian National Congress. An IIM student suggested changing the brand name to Nirodh. To date Nirodh still remains a rather shouty name that makes me laugh.

Sports made me squirm. I was painfully shy in front of the boys. I watched them play football on the field and observed how they got riled up and sometimes broke into a fight. I was not getting a taste of that male aggression simply by not participating in any sport that involved teamwork. The PT teacher could not get me to run a relay race with the boys or include me in a volleyball team. I would disappear during the class. I hung out with the girls in the classroom, who played five stones or blind man's bluff. On Sundays, I played gulli-danda, marbles and badminton with the younger kids, who did not seem like a threat. Seniors and boys in my class had already labelled me a soft, effeminate boy they could never be friends with. The only time I excelled was in a walking race on Sports Day. First prize. I think I walked swiftly like a tawaif ignoring a clingy patron. The other boys complained that I cheated. That I was running. Had they seen a tawaif walk, they would naturally fall by, no? The principal watched me attempt football with my friend Sweta, a tomboy who was better at it than me. She tried teaching me and failed miserably as she scored goal after goal. The principal once again hung his head in shame. He could not fix me.

In class, the teacher asked, What do you want to be when you grow up? A question that shaped many a doctor and an engineer. I struggled. One year I wanted to be a painter. I was sketching women in fancy clothes and jewellery, inspired by a girl in the hostel, Yangtze, who sketched marvellous figures. Next year I wanted to be a fashion designer. I was helping the girls dress up for their fashion-show performances. Everyone stared at me. One year I said a playwright. Everyone stared again. It was a word most had never heard. Creativity seemed more like a curse than a gift. A senior boarder, Sameer, who was considered the most charming and charismatic boy in the hostel, read an essay I was writing about how the incessant rains were ruining crops. He said I should think of rain as the beginning of life, not the end. Gave me perspective. Changed the tonality of my essay. Or the fact that this dishy boy Sameer was asking me how seriously I wanted to be a writer. Dead serious, if I could impress him. I should be a writer. That was it. It stuck. It helped me drift away from schoolbooks and read outside the syllabus—anything that could help me imagine my own stories. Horror stories were a favourite genre to read under the quilt with a torch when the lights went out at night. Satyajit Ray's horror stories. Guy de Maupassant's horror stories. The Ramayana, the Mahabharata, the Jataka Tales, the Panchatantra—as brutal and violent horror stories.

An incident emboldened me to think that I had acquired special powers by staring at the moon when the electricity went out. It was late evening. Kids were playing in the moonlight before dinner. I was sitting on a bench in the garden with a friend, narrating Maupassant's chilling story *The Horla*. There was a room before us with French windows and a spired roof. We could see that it was empty. In the climax of the story, the narrator, who is haunted by an invisible entity, decides to trap the entity in his house and burn it. As he does so, he watches from behind laurel bushes. He sees a flame dart up the sky. He fathoms he has failed and now must kill himself. As I was retelling this, we noticed a beam of light shoot up from inside the room. My victim, the boy who was keenly listening, shrieked and ran away. He thought I could manifest ghosts and spirits. I did not correct him. It was actually a vehicle driving downhill that reflected its headlights in the room's window. What made it worse for the boy was that he went to the toilet to pee in the dark. I followed him and stood in the urinal next to him, saying, What if the light came back just now? It did. He zipped up halfway and ran again. Silly boy. How could the light be scarier than the dark? If anything, I should have been convinced I had acquired the powers of storytelling. With a little wink from the universe.

Boarders lived in the hostel for nine months a year, from March to November, getting a fortnight's vacation for Dussehra and a three-month winter holiday from December to February. The principal often took us on a trek. One time we walked all night to reach Tiger Hill for sunrise. A spectacular sight, no doubt, but even more enchanting when a bunch of kids walked uphill together at night in the moonlight, learning to be unafraid of the dark. We were taken to Mirik lake, the Teesta valley tea garden, the Rumtek monastery, Thimphu and Paro in Bhutan, and Sandakphu, where it was snowing when we reached, giving us a chance to make snowballs and aim for our strict teachers. It was during these treks that I once entered a forest and saw a black pool of water shaded by tall pine trees. It had an eerie stillness, like a painting so calm that it felt like any moment a beast could jump out and lunge at my throat. I do not know why it made me feel serene, yet disturbed. That image has a special frame in my heart. A violence of silence?

My mother arranged for me to be flown from the Bagdogra airport to Calcutta for the Dussehra holidays. This was another first for the school. I was nine when I first sat in a plane. Mother welcomed me with a bouquet of flowers. This was straight out of a movie the first time it happened. Next year she came without flowers. So it is to be understood that only the first time is special. After that, you stop being special.

At the kotha, she showed me off as a cultured, well-mannered, well-behaved English-speaking child. She made me read from my books. *TV mein jaise news padhte hain, waise kar ke dikha*, was her instruction. Read like the news anchors do on television. I did. She clapped. The other tawaifs appreciated with wah-wah and masha allah, touching their ear lobes for good luck, cracking their knuckles on their temples and blessing me. The novelty of reading news soon wore off. It was no talent. Not special at all. It bored me.

*Main toh isse doctor banaungi*, Mother said. I will make him a doctor.

This prompted a tawaif to joke, *Haan, haan, accha hai, humara ilaaj muft mein ho jayega.* He will treat us for free.

Me, a doctor? I had once wailed so hard at the sight of a syringe at a clinic that Mother had to slap me into shock for a blood sample.

That I might become a doctor was not music to my ears—not at the kotha, for sure, where music was shaping my imagination in other professions: a dancer, a singer, a musician, a director, a poet. When Mother looked lovingly at me with her aspirations, I smiled half-heartedly. It was not going to happen. She never asked me what I wanted to become. Parents think in the interests of their child without consulting them. Classic recipe for a monumental failure.

She never invested in my dreams. Were they nightmares? What were my dreams, what did I want to be? I probably would not have clear answers, and that is the point of being a child. I did not know but someone had to poke the curiosity to express.

She dressed me as a mendicant Sufi saint in a Chartreuse green robe, making me call for alms at each door in the kotha. Tawaifs gave raw rice or money. No chocolate. Halloween for saints. Between this and the doctor, I would go with the more dramatic costume of the robe, beads and the headscarf. Toss in an Ali Maula song and dance. It would be perfect.

No one explained anything at the kotha. It was just how it was. For instance, my mother never told me why my father did not live with us. Why I did not have a set of two parents, like the schoolbooks said, a family. I never asked. It never occurred to me. I understood by sight. I saw him come. I saw him leave. She said, *Tere papa aa gaye. Baahar jaa ke khel.* Your father is here. Go out and play. He ruffled my hair and called me beta. I felt acknowledged, accepted. The heavy purdah dropped for what would appear from its thick, still folds that a private communion was under way.

Years ago, after their fight, she had left the city, but now she had to acquiesce. She had returned stronger and firmer in her resolve to not allow her emotions to get in the way of her profession. Bombay made her tougher than she already was. She did not show my father the door when he came with his friends for a mujra. My father was a guest, like the many other patrons visiting the kotha.

Men are welcome, but not as a parent, because they have their own wives and families to return to where they can wield power and control. At the boarding school, children as young as four and five lived without parents for nine months—nine months in their mama's womb and nine months away from her every year hence. Come to think of it, that is rather ironic, cruel or poignant even, depending on how you read it. But it would seem normal if the child were conditioned from such a tender age. Nothing unusual about it. I doubt such children are able to bond with their families more than the friends they choose in school. So then why should it seem odd at the kotha to get only one parent for a bargain?

I had a single mother, but one who was busy working right in front of me. How much of her time was left to love me? Winter months were the peak season. I watched her either sitting with ustads for music riyaaz in the morning, gossiping with the other tawaifs in the afternoon or attending to patrons in the evening.

There was a steady stream of people coming in and out of the kotha. Friends, relatives, a thin man with an even thinner moustache who came with a brown briefcase neatly packed with beautiful silk saris in maroon and yellow as if it was contraband, which he claimed it was. The purest silk from Hong Kong and Japan. Mother touched it as gently as she rubbed it on her cheek, confirming luxury clothing as a drug she occasionally indulged in. Another man came with ruby and emerald jadau and kundan gemstone jewellery from Jaipur and off-white pearls from Hyderabad, an expensive drug she could only indulge in her thoughts. A choodiwallah, bangle seller, walked in, carrying colourful glass bangles on a bamboo pole. Hawkers were selling everything from fruits to vegetables, buddhi ke baal, cotton candy, pink pastry in a trunk, which the children would not miss for a nap; flowers, toys, laundry, all manner of household items. The mall came to us before it came to India. There were some other unique vendors. A mattress maker came with a strange harp-like wooden instrument. He plucked the bowstring that made a vibrating twang sound. It was fascinating to watch him fluff our bedding and pillows with that humming rhythm. A chhuriwala would come only up to the main gate of the kotha to sharpen knives. Bandook Gully, where knives were polished at the entrance, seems just about ideal to be deemed dangerous. Why did he not step in? Could he be trusted with a sack full of knives? If he had knives, the women inside had something scarier: unflinching stares as weapons of combat. I loved watching him pedal to accelerate the speed of a disc on which the knife sang a bristly, hummy tune, sparking fire. A portly Bengali man in a dhoti carried a lumpy bundle of Hindi pulp fiction novels for rent in a dusty, cream bedsheet. These novels had lurid covers and blood-soaked titles such as *Jahannum Ki Apsara*, *Biwi Ka Hathyara*, *Kala Karnama*. The servants of tawaifs cooked, cleaned and washed. A mehtar, janitor came to clean the toilet in the morning. A pandit came to chant an undecipherable mantra and ring a small bell. A bhishti, water bearer, carried water up and down from the haud, water well, in a mashak, a leather bag made from goat skin, twice a day. Beggars came, street singers came, snake charmers came, the madari entertainer came with two monkeys—girlfriend and boyfriend—a little girl balancing the tightrope came, a fortune teller came with his parrot, keeping the kotha buzzing as a fun fair.

Every time Mother had a visitor, she said to me, *Baahar jaa.* Go out. Baahar jaa and do what? Baahar jaa here meant that I was to hang around in the semicircular open space outside the room. I was not to step out of the kotha. Where did I fit in all of this if I was barred from participating in any of her activities? I consoled myself that she had no time for me, and did not disturb her. I began feeling neglected. Who else could fill that void? My father, who else? He should have the time. What does he do staying out? Why does he not come home every day? Visiting home for the holidays increased my yearning to see my father—a consequence of seeing boarders arrive and leave with theirs, once in the beginning and once at the end of the school term. Had I been studying in Calcutta as a day scholar, and if my mother dressed me for school and fetched me in the afternoon, would I have missed my father? Maybe not. I would have seen him occasionally at the kotha. Conversely, I would have had no friends in such a scenario—because how could I tell them where I lived, what my mother did for a living or invite them to the kotha for my birthday party? It is easier to explain my world when I am far away from it.

*Mujhe mere papa se milao,* I said. I want to meet my father. Mother sent me along with a servant to his shop in Macchua Bazaar. *Isse dikha aa iske baap ki manhoos shakal. Laut-te waqt Royal hotal se biryani ke liye paise maang lena,* she said. Show him his father's wretched face. And get money for biryani from the Royal Hotel. *Aur mere liye firni,* I added. A rice pudding for me. We sat in a hand-pulled rickshaw and went to a tin shop. My father was a tin-sheet dealer. I returned home clutching a sweaty, shiny five-rupee nickel coin, proudly showing it to my mother as if I had won a lottery. What she did for me did not amount to the wealth I had just acquired. She did not want to break my heart with the truth about him.

The earliest memory of my father is also the most inextinguishable, violent like a wild forest fire.

A man got out of bed and stood in front of me. A woman sat behind me, adjusting her petticoat, and miraculously switched on the single yellow bulb hanging from the ceiling. I could tell it was my mother from the silvery sounds of her bangles and anklets—the music was home to my ears.

Turning around would have made me catch my mother in the act. I was too groggy to be surprised. Our living space was so tiny, and yet we had to often accommodate an unwelcome guest in bed, even when there was no room for more.

Where was my cot? I did not have one, or we could not afford one—but the easiest explanation for that would be that mothers like mine did not believe in sleeping away from their only child.

But who was this stranger before me—tall, bushy, naked?

He smiled. *Kya dekh raha hai?* What are you looking at?

He stooped to pick his trousers up from the floor and hunched over to wear them. A thick gold chain around his neck glinted in the dim light; his smile grew distinctly creepy as he fumbled with his pants.

Did I stare at his genitals when he questioned me? What was I looking at?

Here was a naked man who had been having sex with my mother a while ago. I was lying next to them, turned away from the sight, but not the sounds. Sound was sight. My ears soaked in metal sounds jangling with huffs and moans to build a rhythm. The sounds of coruscating flesh flung meteoric sparks across my closed eyelids. The two bodies slammed into one another, trying to enter each other, as if a door was shutting in their faces each time they tried to pass. And so they continued indefatigably, sweating and smelling of liquor and fading jasmines.

What I heard was painting pictures. There was a voyeuristic thrill in connecting the senses to a visual performance. Pupils adapt in the dark as they feel the sensations clouding their whites. The heightened senses of sound, touch, smell and taste are what make us inveterate nocturnal mammals, willing to substitute sight in return for its favours.

Who climaxed first?

A silence arose from their clammy loins. Heat escaped into vapour in the room. A stench reached my nose. It had the salty scent of something either sacred or sinful. I could not tell the difference because it was done so sneakily. Thick clouds of frankincense from a ritual hung in the air. Their heavy breaths were taking cognisance of what had transpired in the room. There was no snapping sound of a condom coming off.

The man walked out of the door. The light was switched off. I went back to sleep without a word exchanged between Mother and me. There was no need to. I was certainly not going to remember the incident the next morning, or the one after that—if it happened so often that one recollection was enough to cancel out all the other instances when my bedtime was interrupted by a post-coital kerfuffle.

I believe that is the first time I encountered a naked stranger in my bed. He had a boozy loftiness that comes from knowing too little in the exultant moment, but he did not register to me as a man out of his skin. He smelt like home.

My mother was his mistress. He came for sex. She gave him love. She gave him me, a drowsy child to a father who occasionally shared the only bed we had, and who never kissed us goodnight before he walked out of the door.

A few times he took me out for a walk, bought me chocolate and fulfilled his paternal duties before he attended a mujra. I saw him getting sozzled and singing to my mother during her performance. She would stop and let him take over the mujra, a hirsute tawaif trying to impress her with his slurry rendition of *Mere Mehboob Tujhe Meri Mohabbat Ki Kasam*. His friends fell over themselves to applaud him with resounding claps and whistles. *Wah wah! Wah wah!* He was probably sponsoring their whisky. My mother would often ask her ustads—the men playing the tabla, the baaja, the sarangi—to take a break until he was done. *Party kadki hai,* she would whisper to them. These patrons have no money.

The kotha was open to patrons until midnight. At midnight, a durbaan, guard, would close the entrance. No patron could stay. If a tawaif chose, she would step out with her favoured patron for a late-night dinner and a hotel-room dalliance. The children did not miss their mothers. We were told our mothers had stepped out for dinner or that they had been called to perform at a function in another kotha. We did not suspect anything. We slept and found our mothers in bed when we woke up. Nothing was amiss in our presence. Their absence did not affect us at the boarding school, where we would probably have less time for them if they came to live with us. The tawaifs had no such luxury to devote their lives to raise their child. Someone from their family—a sister, an aunt, a grandma—fostered the child.

Mother was keen to know if I ranked first in class at the end of the final exams, when the report card was sent to her by mail. I had to be the best. There was no second option. She did not know how to read. She asked the Masterji, a teacher who taught tawaifs how to read and write in Hindi, to check the report card. The first few years were fine. After Class 3 she was taken by surprise. It seemed I was distracted. She was upset when Masterji told her I had ranked second or third. The chappal, the comb, the school wooden ruler—any object that could serve a beating—was in her hand. *Main yahaan din raat khatt ke tujhe padha rahi hoon, itna paisa kharcha kar rahi hoon, aur tu fail hota ja raha hai,* she shouted. I am toiling away here day and night, spending so much money on your education and you are failing. I remained quiet, enduring it. She did not understand that the beating severely affected my performance. She thought it was a corrective measure to help me study harder. There was no one to tell her to stop beating her child, and she listened to no one, locking the room to thrash me. My defence was only in my tears. It had little effect on her because she was convinced she was doing the right thing to prevent failure. How was I to know then what her own story of hardship was? Even if she told it to me, how much would I have made sense of it, not treating it as a fable, a bedtime story? In fact, she sang for the world, but not a single lullaby for me.

Once, she tied my hands to the window where I kept the vase with the dying flowers. Jesus Christ in the kotha! Now that I think of it, my legs were crossed too. Such a diva pose! Phullo, our nasty-ass neighbour tawaif, strutted past me, smiling like the devil. Satan! Another time, my mother locked me in the common toilet. Until someone had to use it urgently. I was then moved to the common bathroom. One year, she stripped me bare and made me sob for hours by the stairs. Humiliated and ashamed. She protected me from others, but what about her? Who was going to save me from her? Violence blisters my memory.

*Naazuk bachcha hai,* she said, describing me to strangers. He is a delicate child. Not a special child. Just fragile. And yet, she was raising me with an iron fist. There was no mercy shown. A timid child growing up in an all-woman environment with an ignorant mother who did not understand what naazuk meant. She had had a child only to prove to her detractors that she was not infertile.

But did she know anything about how to raise a child? She told the world how much she loved her naazuk child. That love manifested itself in violence. Do you raise a naazuk child by harming them? What did she mean by naazuk? Was I physically weak? Was I ultra-sensitive? She had only seen girls being raised in her house, except her youngest sibling, an infant Dasrath, whom she did not spend much time with. Did she know how to raise a boy? If you keep calling a boy naazuk, do you not make the bud wilt before it blooms? Her false bravado and her stern hand made me drift away from the only person I was meant to love. I never told her anything about me. My thoughts, my wishes, my desires—I never fostered any, knowing she would not fulfil them. I was naazuk from the outside, but was growing strong and resilient from the inside. It was easy to keel over to the dark side, but with so much glitter and music around me, I must have found a way to thrive without going batshit crazy. Naazuk, that word haunted me like a slur everywhere. People used it as a taunt and made me even more conscious of trying out anything that required grit.

One year, when I ranked first in class, she trunk-called me at the boarding school. I got a Videocon television for you because you stood first in class, she said. But it would take me eight months to be back home to see my prize. I got you a Godrej refrigerator because you stood second, she said the next year. But it would take me almost a year to see it. And what would I do with a fridge anyway? I got you an Akai VCR player for your third rank. But I would not be using it like a video game, would I? Consolation prizes after the beatings, to motivate. I accepted my gifts without pulling out the silk ribbons and bows and tearing shiny boxes. My gifts were too big and useless for me. I would have liked a toy. I would have liked something that could belong to me alone. I did not own a Chinese video game or a Japanese pencil box the kids from Nepal, Bhutan, Bangladesh and Tibet got from their vacations to the boarding school. Sure, my mother sent money to the school for a birthday cake. It was celebrated in school at teatime. Enthusiastic children clapped harder in the hope that they would each get a slice. Not everyone got lucky. But what about me? What did I get from it? What is a birthday without a gift to a child? I was never told that the cake itself was the gift. Would that have made me a wiser kid? I doubt it. The cake was tasty. I got to make new friends for a week. But my mother was physically missing from the celebrations. Every single year. Her trunk call to wish me got my pulse racing, but could it replace her physical presence? At least at the Bombay kotha, I received a house-shaped birthday cake with her holding and guiding my hand clasping a knife. We had a photograph of it in an album. That crooked chocolate house, now in a sepia tint, stands in for a nest that never existed to shelter us together. My mother and I blew out the skinny, tiny melting candles together as quickly as we could, so as not to allow its waxen taste to sour our sweetening bond. It must have been inordinately better to celebrate my birthday with my mother, at home with a crooked chocolate-cake house. In school, the cake began to feel like an obligation. It began to taste the same as the cake from the year before, sweet and avoidable. It began to embarrass me. What was the need to celebrate something that all the children had in common? After my mother started the trend of having my birthday celebrated at the hostel, kids told their parents to send money for cake. The trend caught on. It was no longer a special occasion. It felt like being singled out, as I grew taller and resentful. I found all of it quite unnecessary. I did not want to be in the spotlight. I was not doing well with my scores, so it felt even more glaringly ugly to put me in the hot seat. I stopped eating cake.

# The Nineties

MY MOTHER'S FINAL MUJRA WAS FOR MY FATHER. IT WAS THE FINAL one I remember watching. When my father spotted me peeping from the purdah, he grabbed me and sat me down beside him. Mother stopped singing her ghazal and asked me to leave by arching an eyebrow.

Let him stay, my drunk father slurred.

She stared at me. I knew that look. A tawaif's greatest indignity is her own son becoming her patron. I would have happily performed an opening act for her mehfil. She was raising me independent and freethinking, but she remained unconscious of it because she was playing the traditional mother role first. I fled with a handful of nuts and half a bottle of soft drink in my hand. It was my father's way of saying, *Ja baahar ja ke khel.* Go out and play. There was nothing out of the ordinary in her performance. I must have ruined her mood.

She would have to find me a boy my age to hang out with outside the kotha, someone she could trust with my safety.

A tawaif had sent her children to Dr Graham's Homes in Kalimpong. Another had sent her child to Goethals Memorial School in Kurseong. There were two Meena bais at the kotha. One lived next door, and the other, who was dark and thin, lived downstairs. This skinny Meena had two children—a girl, Rimjhim, who went to Loreto School in Calcutta, and an older boy, Sunny, whom she wanted to move from a local school to Darjeeling.

My mother helped the skinny Meena admit her son in my school by saying we were related. I was elated! Excuse the rhyme. I was going to have a sibling, a brother. Finally, someone to call my own. We were in the same class as well. Class 6. Initially, I bossed over him, proudly showing him off to everyone as my brother, even though our surnames did not match. Sunny had a Marwari surname. How is he your brother? Some kids asked. I clarified to those perplexed. Not by blood, I said, far cousin. Far as me living upstairs and he downstairs at the kotha. It felt so good to know I was not alone any more. I tried to include him in everything. I found him to be the polar opposite of me. He would not enter the library. He did not talk to girls. He did not write essays, sketch dresses, pluck daisies or pick leaves of the sour thotne plant and eat it when hungry. How very disappointing! He was obsessed with cricket. He bought the whole gear—bats, balls, wickets, knee pads, ball guard, helmet, white T-shirt and trousers. He made it look professional. He formed teams and took over the only ground where kids played football, volleyball, badminton and kho-kho, as long as they secured a corner. Now this became a bit of a tussle for the sporty kids. Sunny hustled and found more kids to try the new sport. Soon, I lost out on the brother I had hoped would be my tail. Sunny was not good at studies. It was a very brief brotherly relationship, I must say. He left the school the next year or after, I do not remember, but by then he had become so inconspicuous a brother that I gave up on him without a fight. It did not occur to me that perhaps he did not want to be seen with me. I was the sissy boy pretending to be his older, protective brother. He did not need me the way I did.

I reimagined *Cinderella* into a play called Cinderarchie for Founder's Day. No one wanted the main role. I took the part, mopping and sweeping the floor and washing clothes—household chores boys were not taught to do. It must have been an uncommon sight to watch, more a source of practical joke to kids watching me rehearse it. According to their titters, I was enacting my wildest fantasies. In the play, I lose my working boot at the ball. A girl named Manisha took on the part of Princess Charming, who proposes. Will you marry me? she asked. The audience stared for my answer on the makeshift stage shoddily erected on the football field. Manisha asking Manish that all-important, life-altering question. I am not making this up. I froze. I forgot my line. One word. I was supposed to say yes. I believe it was this exact moment, still as bright and reflective as that luminous day in June that makes me squint even now in its harsh glare. I knew this was not for me. Stage, acting, lying by saying yes, spotlight. I managed a feeble yes. Yes, I was different from everyone. Yes, I was never going to be accepted for it. Yes, I should disappear into the shadows. The curtain dropped on my promising career on stage. I stopped putting up my name for quizzes, extempores, elocutions and poetry recitals—things I previously and actively participated in to avoid sports. The stage was an outlet to express and get out of my comfort of wanting to remain invisible. I grew into even more of an introvert.

On a Sunday afternoon, when it was raining, the boys were instructed to remain indoors in the dormitory and read in bed. Vaibhav occasionally slept with me in the dormitory. Our marriage was a secret that had now evolved into an affair. Today, he slid into my quilt in full view of all the other students in the room. I did not mind it. I was turned to one side, reading. He was turned to the other side, playing with himself. Now, this I had not noticed because it was daytime, and everyone in the room was awake and alert. I thought my husband was dozing. A boy named Jason descended from his upper bunk and pulled our quilt away, exposing Vaibhav's hard dick in his hand. Everyone laughed. Vaibhav said he was preparing to fuck me. What? No. I thought we only did such things in the night time, sneakily. No, no, no, no, no, this was a lie. This was not true. We had not planned on having sex like this in the afternoon, in full view of all the other boarders in the room. Vaibhav, being the alpha male that he projected himself to be, got up and walked away, shrugging and cursing Jason for killing his mojo. Everyone stared at me as if I were the coy bride abandoned on her suhaag raat, wedding night. Typical of me to use that expression just as well. After all, we had role-played as husband and wife earlier. When the students went out for tea, I stayed in, unable to move from my bed. I was guilty, shamed and now exposed to the carnal desires of all the boys in the room. I could feel the heat of their eyes on my body. Every single one of them. Word spread. Older students then routinely began creeping into my bed at night. Some I consented to, some I resented, whispering my own umms and nos, but I could not tell anyone. I could not shout or yell. If a student snitched, I would be punished, and maybe even expelled. I was playing exclusively with the girls in the daytime and playing even more of a dangerous game with the boys in the dark. The teachers were, in any case, uniformly telling me to behave like a boy and play sports, and not spend all my time in the library, playing antakshari with the girls, blah, blah, blah. And here I was now, a postman for love letters between the two sexes. Satisfying the sexual curiosity of the boys, who wrote long missives, sometimes dictated by me, that should have been written for me.

Teasing got punny. The principal was teaching us *Julius Caesar* in the period after lunch, when I usually dozed off. He used to refer to me as the class's sleeping beauty. Giggle, giggle.

He read out Cassius's speech:

*But, woe the while, our fathers' minds are dead,*
*And we are governed with our mothers' spirits.*
*Our yoke and sufferance show us womanish.*

Some kid in the back bench repeated the last word 'womanish' as two words. Wo-manish. Giggle, giggle. All eyes turned to me. Wake up, wo-manish! The principal had spoken. Wo-manish caught on as a dirty word to catch my attention and laugh. I thought it was rather ingenious. I was being taunted in Shakes-speak. Tersely, those three lines do reflect the trium of my father, mother and me.

Teasing did not rattle me. But bullying, using physical force, harming me—that was something I found other ways to deal with. This may have been something I picked up from my observation at the kotha, where women do not react to insults but fight back when it comes to blows. A boy named Pratik argued with me. He could not win. I was good at insults. My aggression was passive, challenging my opponent to harm me. I'll cut your ear with this blade, he said, flashing it in front of the students in a study hall. I dare you, I said. He nicked my ear. I did not move. It bled but I did not cry. I did not retaliate. Everyone saw that I endured bloodletting. Pratik realized his mistake and apologized. He could be worse off if this got reported. He never troubled me again. He tried inviting me to sleep with him later, but that, too, was never going to happen. Another time a boy tried to physically bully me in the dormitory. I grabbed his neck and pressed hard till he choked. He never messed with me again. With another boy, I rammed my head into his belly when he tried to punch me. I did not think of being violent. I did not practise my moves. I reacted instinctively to protect myself from further harm, as the tawaifs at the kotha did. They did not spend all day learning martial arts. Yet, the slender hand could turn stern in defence.

A heady cloud of sinful sex, shame, teasing—social pariah was setting in. I was being singled out as the aberrant one. I could sense the internalization of my conscience, building up from instinct, to the reaction of the people around me. Instinct to be just me, or was it something else? Was I giving in? I was never a bad student. I studied diligently, like the others. I did not understand how I was going from bad to worse.

A new cycle became commonplace. I went home with poor grades, the beatings continued. I returned to school for a new year, performing worse. My mother could not own her childhood. She tried to correct it through me. Before she could even bond with me, her fears came in the way. My grandmother, Gullo, had lugged me around. Shanna Mausi, Babna Mausi, Hasina Mausi, Rajjo Didi, Laxmi Didi, Uma Tai and Usha Tai were around at various stages of my first seven to eight years, when Mother was at her peak. Mother must have meant more to them than she did to me. I was yet to recognize and decorate her as a hero for her valour.

A worse calamity awaited. A boy whose advances I had spurned told the principal that I was entertaining boys at night. We were watching a movie in the recreation hall when the principal arrived and called me out, saying I was spoiling the boys and would be moved to a new hostel building with the younger kids. Kids murmured in the hall and stared at me. I was the vamp. Adding to my woes, a girl peeped into a classroom and saw me playing with a friend, tripping and falling on him on the floor, which she interpreted as sex and reported. A true menace. The principal called me into his office and said he was going to call my mother and inform her that I was doing dirty, filthy things. It traumatized me. Made me go mute. My grades spiralled.

It was the year my mother chose to introduce a new father. She brought her new beau, Kothari, to my boarding school. She asked me if I wanted to call him my papa.

But he is not my papa, I said.

What was she thinking? She was not. How was she trying to pass him off as my new dad? We did not even look alike.

That weekend, they took me to town for an outing. They shared a bed in a hotel room. I was tucked on a couch by a window. There were tremors from an earthquake. I woke up in the middle of the night to see their bed shaking. I thought it was them shaking the earth with their unbridled passion. I then saw a lamp fall, a chair move. The light went out in the window. But they remained glued inside a fat quilt. Not even an earthquake could swallow that horrendous man.

On the prickly subject of my father's relationship status with us, Mother added the term 'late' before his fake name, Anoop. It was something we discussed briefly when she showed Kothari around the school premises. *Koi poochhe toh kehna marr gaye*, she conspiratorially whispered. If someone asks, say he died. *Kaise*, I asked. How? Heart attack, she said blithely. Heart attack, I repeated plainly, deceiving no emotion.

I called Kothari Uncle. Resentfully. I knew him as a patron. I had seen him at the kotha. He was a regular. I had sensed he was becoming a favourite—of hers, not mine. He was a tall, slim, dark man with an oily smile. I did not find anything likeable about him, unlike the hauteur I noticed in my father's deep voice that made him somewhat of an alluring figure. Kothari was cranky. He had no sophistication in his querulous voice, dressing or manners. He had a perpetual scowl on his face; ridges formed on his forehead like exclamation marks had collapsed in straight, horizontal lines at his exasperating thoughts. Back home at the kotha, he, too, had noticed me draping my mother's shawls and dupattas and dancing effeminately, cavorting with Bunny. He despised it. He instigated Mother, saying her naazuk boy was a sissy. He was extremely opinionated and judged hastily. Watching me as a young boy undulating his hips to the sound of the pungi in the melody *Yaara*

*Sili Sili*, a bai, Meera said, *Apni mummy ki lachak hai.* He has his mother's sinuous moves. My mother carried the ebb and flow of the waves in her kamar, waist. I was elated to be compared to her. Kothari said boys did not dance.

His entry into her life was the turning point for me to exit from hers.

Mother began parroting his lines when he was around. Everything he said was right for her. I saw them fucking. It disgusted me. Before this, I had seen my mother get intimate only with my father. I was a kid then. I found no reason to compartmentalize their coupling into my memory as an unsightly or unnatural act. But this Kothari chap was ugh. Slimy guy. I had my reservations. They were allowed to fornicate freely and I could not even shake a leg? I begrudged them with silent fury. They drank whisky and had sex quite often. There was a sharp drop in patrons. Favoured patrons had only recently been coming to the kotha for sex as the mujra had stopped. The landlord, Putput, was clamping down on the tawaifs to evict them. Rooms that were usually draped with a purdah were now latched from the inside. I had the adjacent small room, separated by a flimsy sliding door. I heard sounds. I saw things no child should be privy to when the door was sometimes carelessly left open. One time, my mother invited me to sit in the room and watch television when it was cold outside. She sat behind me, wrapped in a quilt. Kothari fondled her under it. I found the whole thing repulsive. I could see their shenanigans show up each time the screen in front of me went black, reflecting what they were doing behind my back. I wept, pretending to concentrate only on the television screen showing Dev Anand and Nutan singing and dancing to the melody *Chhod Do Aanchal Zamana Kya Kahega*. I found a *Debonair* magazine under the mattress. Condoms. In a role reversal, I was the child discovering ugly truths about my careless mother. I mean, she was being careful with protection, but careless with attention.

Phullo's son, Ajay, introduced me to untapped desires. It was New Year's Eve. He asked my mother if I could sleep in his room, along with his elder brother. We were watching a late-night movie. She was hesitant but Kothari permitted. He wanted to have our room for himself and Mother. Ajay was tall, fair and handsome. Uday snored on one side. Ajay kissed me and cuddled with me on one end of the large bed. I liked it. I was used to it. It was what boys did with me in the hostel in Darjeeling. It was gentle. It was consensual. This was also the first time I should say I wet myself. My crotch was wet with a sticky substance. I woke up in the morning with a stiff front in my underwear. I guess I ushered in the New Year with a new discovery about myself! I was immediately infatuated with Ajay. We snogged at every opportunity, on the pretext of studying in a room, or watching *Chitrahaar* together, or when the mothers were out. Years went by like this—I returned to the kotha for my winter vacation, just as he and his brother and sister did from Kalimpong. Ajay and I found ways to sneak into each other's rooms to kiss and fondle. We found the dark, unlit corridor leading to the toilet a great place to make out. Once, when everyone was asleep—when my mother was under the influence of alcohol, and his mother under the influence of too much late-night television—he snuck into my room, pulled my pyjamas down and put my penis into his mouth. It felt good, but this was new. We had never done this before. How is it so fresh? he asked. I giggled. I took a bath before bedtime, I said. This also meant that now I would have to put his penis into my mouth. He was a big guy, me petite. But what the hell! I eventually got there after some coaxing. We even tried putting our penises into each other's buttocks. I am not sure how far we got, but, oh, did we try passionately! Not something I thought I could pull off, or, rather, put in. But I enjoyed it. It made me feel I did not have to always be the naazuk, gentle, submissive, receiving kind. I could also be the giver. I am using these quaint expressions because back in the day we did not know what it meant to be queer, or if we were topping or bottoming. We were, however, having a great time exploring each other's bodies. But Ajay moved on quickly from teenage fun to playing adult. He wanted to be a dude bro like his elder sibling, Uday. He got a bike. Then one heard he got a girlfriend. He wanted to get married, start a family and make babies.

One chapter closing always opened the next. Skinny Meena's son, Sunny, and I began snogging, but it was brief and ended when he took me to Karnani Mansion with a few other friends he had made outside the kotha. We were at a brothel. A madam showed us beds separated by white curtain sheets in a room. Each bed had a lady waiting with a lurid smile on her face. It made me uncomfortable. Sunny was smoking and nudging me to pick a girl. I realized he had grown up. I was not enough for him. Boys outgrew me by sixteen. I walked out, leaving him to it. Ultimately, all said and done, a girl was always the real thing. I simply could not compete with that.

Mother divided her time with that arrogant, loud man Kothari between the kotha and her flat, where she put him up. He arrived at the kotha in the evening. They chatted, drank and had sex. He left at midnight. When did she have the time for me? They took me out for dinner to a glitzy restaurant called Rang Mahal during a festive occasion. He whispered to the waiter to mix whisky with Thums Up for my mother. A classic combo. She sipped on it through a straw, pretending it was unadulterated like my bottle of orangey Gold Spot. I was no fool.

At home, when she beat me for low grades once, I pulled out a bottle of Royal Challenge from the cabinet and said, If you stop this, I will get the grades.

All right, she said.

She lied. My grades did not improve either.

I spent all my time poring over the works of Maugham and Marquez—I fairly doubt I ever completed even one book. I mainly carried them around like a clutch, an accessory to my intelligence. I was writing letters to my mother filled with lyrics of Hindi film songs. Instead of writing a formal question—How is the weather?—I wrote, *Yahaan ka mausam badaa haseen hai, phir bhi jaan udaas hai*, echoing the words of *Kabootar Ja Ja Ja* from *Maine Pyar Kiya*. My imagination was sprouting wings to escape the oppressive boarding-school environment. When the letters stopped coming, she telephoned me and said, *Tu toh badaa angrez ka choda ho gaya hai re, chitthi bhi nahi likhta.* What an English prick you have become, you don't even write to me any more! What could I say to that? What do you say to a person who does not reply to your letters? On a trunk call that lasts no more than a minute. I was embarrassed by my home address: Bandook Gully. I imagined it must have been called Bandhu Gully originally. I translated it from Bengali to Friend's Lane. The postman lost his way.

On the weekend, when the principal put out the week's newspapers on a bench by the school bell, I developed a habit of reading *The Telegraph* cover to cover. Franz Kafka's face haunted me in one of the stories. He had the most piercingly clear eyes I had seen. His photo was small, his aura immense. I found his novel *The Castle* in the library. I tried reading it but found it cryptic and boring. Marquez's *Love in the Time of Cholera* and Maugham's *The Painted Veil* suited my spleen. I took an interest in the poems of Shelley and Christina Rossetti, having previously recited Edward Lear's *The Owl and the Pussy-Cat* on stage. I was particularly fond of Rossetti's poem *When I Am Dead, My Dearest.* It may have something to do with me once visiting a cemetery and reading beautiful epitaphs on tombstones, copying them in a notebook and attempting to write my own poetic lines that are now unworthy of a revisitation. A senior girl had read Philip Roth's novel *Portnoy's Complaint* and raved about it, saying it was probably too adult for my age. I felt challenged and read it. I found it humorous, scandalous even; not sure I understood the

Jewish humour, but the explicit language and frank treatment of sexuality resonated with my inner turmoil.

There was no culture of reading at the kotha. To be precise, no culture of reading English literature. It was not the ideal place to read because of the steady stream of interruptions. But if I could do it secretly in a crowded boarding school, I could do it anywhere. So I devoured comics and gossip magazines like fast food. I read discarded books and newspapers from a raddi shop in Bandook Gully like a moth drawn to light. I used my meagre pocket money to read instead of buying a snack. Words seemed to nourish my soul. It helped me deal with the chaos both inside and outside. The Bengali travelling librarian, who wore a dhoti and carried his stash in a dusty white cloth bundle on his shoulder, supplied racy titles to the women at the kothas. I read anything he offered in English, which was not a great selection, but the *Tinkle* comics, the *Chandamama* and *Champak* magazines sufficed. Once, he pulled out a comic that turned out to be a gay porn magazine. Hard-core action! My eyes popped out. *Yeh tumhare kaam ki cheez hai*, he said. This one is up your alley. Which was even more shocking. He knew. How the hell? At first I hesitated. He insisted I take it for a week. I was scared, but also nervous and excited. He did not tell a tawaif. I was still a teen. I think he was smart. He did not want to be banned from the kotha. Why harm his own business? I kept the porn magazine with me for a few months. I learnt a lot from reading its splashy pictures.

I once read a short story titled *The Bet* by Anton Chekhov. It was about a lawyer who accepts a bet with a banker to serve house arrest for fifteen years. A bag full of money awaits him at the end of the term. He stays locked indoors, reads books and, upon his release, forfeits the cash for the wisdom he has gained instead. His renunciation is sullied; haters jealously guard their own ignorance by excoriating him as a bloody fanatical son of a bitch, loosely to be interpreted as randi ka beta in Russian. The story had a powerful impact on me. My cash prize was embedded in the text. I read like the lawyer, writing about what I saw from inside my fortress, the kotha. I began writing a daily diary at the age of sixteen. Late, some would say for my age. During the day, we listened to ghazal riyaaz and the sound of women practising kathak. By evening, I would begin to translate the lyrics, observing in Hindi and expressing in English.

About the stigma surrounding me, I cannot be certain of what I felt, because I had not yet grasped how to fully express my feelings, when, in one of the earliest diary entries I wrote briefly: I am always made to feel like a haraami, a person out of wedlock, a bastard. But it never rattles me because I choose to believe there is more to me than insults. They'll fade away, the bullies, like the banker in *The Bet*.

To hell with randi ka beta! Writing was breaking shackles. Truth loitered over to hear me out. Like the reading lawyer in *The Bet*, I was all of them or none—depending on how I chose to evolve in my words: Shaitaan Ka Beta, Jungle Ka Beta, Alladin Ka Beta, Randi Ka Beta.

Conversations with Mother became more clipped with age, both from her side and mine. She was in thrall of her beau Kothari, who was going to make everything perfect. I did not agree with her. I thought he would be like the other men. My father had used her—her body, her money, her jewellery. She allowed it in the hope that he would eventually become hers. Some bais had left the kotha and settled in the suburbs as mistresses. Kothariji, as she called him, or Veeru, short for his first name Virendra, was just another patron in the same mould as my father. He was using her, and would soon dump her and disappear. He was no Veeru like Dharmendra in *Sholay*, for sure. She often rejected the good ones for the lousy ones. She had a great taste for losers. Despite that, my affection for my father stemmed from my ignorance of his life outside the mujra mehfil. When I saw my mother with Kothari, I wished she were with my real father instead. I was too young to understand what must have transpired between my parents, and too naïve to enquire about it. In school, when I had to lie about his death, I did it without thought. Kothari's entry made me question my father's fake untimely death. Why did he have to die? It bothered me to see the happy parents of other kids and then see my own mother trying to fill the lack of a father figure in my life with a terrible stand-in. Kothari widened the chasm between mother and son. She had to be operated on for some complications in her uterus. He was going to be there at the hospital. She asked me if I would come to see her. I said no. He is there, why do you need me?

When Mother was upset with me, she would switch to the respectful pronoun 'aap' to address me. That is when I knew something was off. At times, we did not speak for a month or more. When she used 'tum' or 'tu', informal addresses for 'you', was when she had cooled down. Another way was her singing *Tum Se Badhkar Duniya Mein Na Dekha Koi/ Aur Zubaan Par Aaj Dil Ki Baat Aa Gayi*, when she wanted me to run an errand. That song was not to flatter, but to hint at the title of the film the song was from: *Kaamchor*, or a lazy person who avoids hard work. It made me laugh and cracked the icy vibes.

On 16 March 1993, a bomb blast in Bowbazar wiped out the kothas. After the demolition of the Babri Masjid in Ayodhya on 6 December 1992, a meticulously planned retaliation attack on 12 March 1993, orchestrated by gangster Dawood Ibrahim, killed hundreds and wounded more than a thousand people in Mumbai. Twelve bombs ripped through the city's gut in a single day. A similar plan was being hatched for the commercial district of Calcutta, Badabazar. Four days after the Bombay blasts, bombs were being stocked in a building's basement in Bowbazar. The alleged mastermind was satta don Rashid Khan, who himself came from a tawaif family and had close ties with several tawaifs living and working in the area, including my mother, who once took me along to meet him when Phullo smashed our radio one morning with a police baton. His men were careless in storing the explosives. Two of them accidentally detonated the bombs. The blast damaged two buildings and killed fifty people, injuring another hundred, although the real numbers are said to be higher. Bais packed up and fled Bowbazar. Rashid Khan's henchmen, rival gangs, all of them were patrons. The tawaifs feared being linked to the goons. They did not want their patrons to be replaced by patrol. Policemen were visiting the kothas, interrogating women and looking for criminals. Regular patrons stopped attending mujras for fear of being unnecessarily harassed. The only music haunting the tram line in Bowbazar were sirens. The ustads who sat in the tea shops dispersed, many migrated to Bombay to look for work in orchestras. Some of the bais began joining the dance bars on Mira Road, Bombay. Some moved to the suburbs in Calcutta, where rich patrons kept them as their second wife.

On Founder's Day in June 1994, when the students of Class 10 performed a Nepali folk dance on stage, boys were paired with girls, and so was I. The choreography was simple, hopping on one foot in the front to an even simpler madal drumbeat. Pairs stood one behind another, in two or three rows. I convinced my partner to stand in the last row with me, to avoid focus. I was so disinterested in the performance that I danced clumsily. For the first time, I was embarrassed to be on stage, doing something I had enjoyed for so long and which now felt like I had to shed to form a more rounded, manly character for myself. Everyone was watching. I had to play the boy for the girl dancing with me. Poor girl—if I danced like a girl, would she be branded a lesbian? Dancing like a boy can be a bit like moving like an oaf. That did not come naturally to me. I was dancing to fail. I was convincing myself, and the spectators watching, that dancing was not for me. This was my final, unimpressive performance as a prodigious nautch boy. If only the tawaifs were watching, they would know what I was doing to blend in, to be common, invisible.

In the final exams, I ranked last in Class 10. The principal mocked me in the assembly by mentioning it out loud. There was no redemption for me. Walking on fire or snow would have been the same. For the ICSE board exams, boarders had to spend their final vacation at the hostel, preparing for it. There were two girls and seven boys in our batch. We spent three months in Yangdoma's house sitting around a chulha, stove, sipping tea and petting Kanchi's pups. The principal, for a special beating, singled me out. He was certain I would fail and bring dishonour to the school's unblemished record. The other students watched in silence as he used a cane. Or was it a belt? I stared blankly at the maths exam paper. I knew I would not score more than ten marks—certain that I would fail but confident that I would pass in all the other subjects. My batchmates were planning to move to new cities for studies. I said I was done being away from home. The train I took from New Jalpaiguri, my first train journey alone, made me feel bold for a new beginning. I opened the door of the moving train and put my head out in the wind, trying to smell freedom in the morning's first warm rays, when suddenly I was hit. Someone had hurled a stone from the passing green fields. It flew like a slingshot aimed at my crotch. I choked on my breath. I felt one of my testicles jump into my stomach. I returned to my seat, breathless. So this is what freedom meant, huh? I reached home, feeling grown up and hurt. As I bent my head to enter my mother's room, Phullo's older son Uday sneaked up from behind me and coloured my face green. *Holi hai!* he greeted me. Ugh, what a messy new life, I thought. I hated Holi at the kotha. Women cooked kheer, halwa, aloo ki subzi and poori early morning on the festive occasion and spent the afternoon dragging each other to the wet floor, smothering each other's faces with gulaal and forcefully stuffing powders in all the colours of the rainbow into their blouse, inside their petticoat, wherever their hands could slide. I looked on in horror, feeling more violated than these women who laughed and joked and seemed to be having fun. Some patrons came by and it got even more riotous. It scarred me. I refused to play, hiding behind a purdah and waiting for Mother to behave so that we could sit down and enjoy our festive meal in peace and quiet.

By 1995, most tawaifs had left the kotha one after another since the Bowbazar bomb blast. Meera, Baby, Gauri, Mallika, Kamandal, Suman, Jhumki, Geeta and the squat Meena had all left. The skinny Meena downstairs, Phullo, Krishna and my mother were the only four remaining. Soon, my mother gathered everyone for my birthday. No birthday gift. I had returned home—that was in itself my biggest gift. I went to meet my father. He was working in his shop. I bought a cake and said, It is my birthday today, please have some. He asked me to keep it on the table by the door. He came over to me, pulled out his wallet and handed me a fifty-rupee note and turned to walk away. I banged the note on his table and said, I did not come here for your money. I left in anger. I did not feel the urge to see him again. It was not hatred. It could not have been love, or I would have forgiven him and tried to rekindle our bond. What bond? We did not have any. We miss only those we love. When he was never around for love, what difference would his absence make? I became indifferent to him, like Mother had mastered.

I spent most days writing letters to my school friends Sweta and Pooja. I began looking around with new eyes as a sixteen-year-old on the brink of adulthood. Phullo's sons Uday and Ajay were running a dingy video-game parlour in the basement of a building in the area. Skinny Meena's drunkard brother Chaman had opened a video-rental library next to the dhobi shop in a narrow lane in the mohalla. I often went there with a tall stainless-steel glass to fetch chai for my mother in the evenings from a popular singara-kachori shop. A youthful electrician worked next to the library. He smiled at me. I smiled back. At another motor repair shop, another young man smiled at me. I smiled back. A curly-haired young paanwala smiled at me. I reciprocated. A news stall owner flirted. I lowered my eyes in sharam, shyness. They smiled even more. It worked like a language without words. I was back at the kotha for good now. When the mujras had all but wrapped up. So were these men now smiling to be invited over for sex? Who did they want to have sex with? Our mothers, or us? I noticed a new boy, tall, dark, naturally handsome by that classic definition, at least to me. Phullo's eldest son Uday had cat-green eyes and a foreigner friend. An old British man, pink as a pig. The old man had picked up a Mallu boy from Kerala and was paying Uday to keep him with them. They rechristened the Mallu boy Vicky. Vicky's height made him look older, but we must have probably been just a few years apart. There was gossip that Uday was the Angrez's blue-eyed boy. The firang had the Mallu boy as a snack. Phullo did not freak out because the payment was in pounds. She pretended that she did not know anything about the firang's noble intentions with the Mallu boy or with her own adult son. She swished up and down the kotha, announcing she was using her favourite 'Chinaal' perfume. Her mispronunciation of Chanel succinctly defined her notoriety. The Mallu boy hardly spoke. He was always listening to a Walkman. My mother took pity on him for no reason. *Bechara, bhookha hoga.* Poor thing, must be hungry. She decided to send him food when no one was looking. Phullo treated Vicky like a slave—talked rudely to him, made the boy run her personal errands and asked him to sleep on the floor in a room where her other children slept on a huge bed. The British man was in London. He visited them once or twice a year. He thought he was Mother Teresa, or that Phullo had a kind heart to give Vicky shelter. She behaved like a guileless nun in his presence. She spent all morning sleeping, all day tweezing her eyebrows and all night watching reruns of *Biwi Ho Toh Aisi* on the late-night Zee Movies cable channel, perhaps taking notes on how not to be a dutiful housewife. She also had a teenage daughter, whose good looks would soon become their own undoing. Mother told me not to speak to Vicky to avoid suspicion. Phullo would pick on anyone to pass her time. I made cow eyes and smiled at Vicky. He smiled back.

So this is what it meant to have agency inside the kotha. I liked him. I made the first move. I expressed to him in my lustful gaze that I wanted to be under him. Ahem, before amen. He picked up the clue like a thoroughbred. What my mother was doing with her man, Kothari, I surreptitiously wanted for myself—a man of my choice. In my earlier experiences, it was always the boys who picked me. I went along without a fuss. Here, I was acting on my own instinct, my desire.

Pona, the landlord Putput's younger brother, befriended me. He asked me to meet him outside. He patiently listened to me talk about school and books. One day, when my mother was not around, he invited me to his room. He said he wanted me to play with his toddler. His wife was away at her parents' house as she was pregnant with his second child. Not suspecting any foul play, I entered his room and looked at his baby in the crib, when suddenly he grabbed me from behind. He pulled my pyjamas down. I felt his penis on my back. I struggled to get away when he pushed me towards a pillar and tried to thrust it in. My buttocks squirmed in resistance. I pushed away with my buttocks, pulled up my pants and ran. It was a narrow escape. I could not tell my mother about this. I thought it would bring further shame upon me, a naazuk boy.

I then spent most of my time inside the kotha, babysitting the children of skinny Meena's extended family. Krishna bai's young son had seen his mother having sex regularly with a patron. She pretended she was giving the patron a hot-oil massage in her tiny room. The boy was aroused. He insisted on sitting on my lap. My mother noticed the kid was sexually curious. She stopped me from playing with him. I was surrounded by sex in my adolescent years. The kotha was turning into a brothel, where kids did what they saw adults do. When the purdahs fluttered in a gust of wind, children saw flashes of intimacy between patrons and their mothers, which fuelled their curiosity.

The ICSE results arrived at home later that year. I had passed with the lowest grades. Mother did not raise her chappal. She thought the exercise would be futile now. She could guide me, or so she thought. She resigned it to: *Chalo, pass toh ho gaya na.* At least he has passed. *Ab science padhna, haan?* Study science now, okay? She called my father and asked him to accompany us to St. Xavier's College. I insisted on Arts. They would not listen to me. The college rejected me on one look at my grades. I was relieved. I found admission in Maulana Azad College, but after a few days switched to St. Paul's Cathedral Mission College. Maulana Azad was an all boys' environment. It made me queasy. I should have been happier having all the boys to myself. With the girls at St. Paul's, no one would pay attention to me. I wanted to go unnoticed. I had trouble understanding the Bengali language, the people and the environment.

College years are a blur. I recall a friend or two, especially a handsome hockey player who liked hanging out with me, perhaps because I was the closest that he, the shy type, could get to a girl. I was fair and shy and had a feminine voice. A queer boy is a harmless introduction to womanhood. I was attracted to him but did not know if I was supposed to express it. I eventually never did. Nor did he. We skipped classes and went to New Empire and Lighthouse to watch *Dunston Checks In* and *Rumble in the Bronx*. We laughed in the corridors of the Indian Museum and ate bhel puri in the Victoria Memorial gardens. Nothing spectacular was happening in my life at home either. Mother had put me up for computer classes at Aptech in Park Street. I went there, met Nikhil, a Marwari boy, who hated it. We spent our time watching movies, hanging out in cafés and waiting outside his girlfriend's college. He was funny, charming and generous. I mustered up the courage to tell him about my background, and took him home. He met my mother. He did not judge me and, instead, invited me to his house to have dinner with his family. That was an actual start to finding my place in the outside world. Not everyone was going to react to me with an ulterior motive.

I saw an advertisement in *The Asian Age* for a writer's workshop for youngsters and convinced my mother to fund my Sunday sessions. There, I learnt the basics, writing a news feature, an essay on radio inventor Marconi—misspelt as Macaroni—and a fiction piece for the workshop journal, imagining an interview with Madonna under Calcutta's monsoon skies. These were baby steps, dreams I nursed, hoping they would lead me to The Statesman House. Its grand white facade, portico and colonnaded verandah captivated me as I queued in the blistering heat to pay the electricity bill at CESC House, itself a striking Art Deco gem across the street. But my dreams stretched further—to The Oberoi Grand, its sprawling Neoclassical facade and pillared entrance throwing out air-conditioned breeze that chilled my sweaty bones. I halted, yearning to step inside, but dared not. I felt too small, not rich enough for its manicured driveway of soft lights and lush palm fronds. Seeking another path, I visited Salt Lake to pick up a hotel management course form, but the exorbitant fees stopped my mother cold. I saw two futures—a writer or a service industry worker. My soft, polite voice was suited for its docile role, like my personality. I would not shout across a street, or even across rooms, to catch someone's attention. I would wait for the traffic to pass, only to find they had already left, unseen. Yet I kept writing. It felt like an urge to get down from a train when it suddenly stopped in a field so quiet, so beautiful, it must be perfect to start afresh. I trusted those baby steps would one day put stride in my walk and carry me closer to my dreams.

Mother had switched to a colour-making business in her flat. Kothari had inveigled himself into her flat and had become a house pest, if you ask me. The colours were making her go blind. She had begun wearing sindoor in her hair, and a mangalsutra. My mother Rekha was becoming like the heroine Rekha. A hilarious delusion. In the morning, Mother and her old maid, whom we called Buaji, prepared a big, fat tiffin at the kotha. Kothari was vegetarian. A red flag. Mother went to her flat and sat with a bunch of housewives from the building in one room, mixing coloured powders in a tub, weighing, packing and handing it over to a salesman to sell in Barabazar. The powders were used to dye threads. This daily routine meant she had a nine-to-five job. She returned to the kotha in the evening before Kothari came around for their evening drinks. She spent her weekends in the flat. So not only was I alone in the kotha all day, I had it to myself on the weekends. What was I going to do with so much freedom? I could not bring my college friends home. Technically, I could not make friends because of the infamy attached to the kotha. Unlike the boarding school, the kotha was too close to a lie. And now my mother was never there for me when I returned from my chaudah saal ka vanvaas, fourteen years of exile, at the boarding school. She was working to provide for me. I did not see it like that. I saw her having a good time with her lover and neglecting her child. I was a teenager—how else was I supposed to understand if she was not going to bond with me? Our teenage years are our most corruptible age. The most violent years.

Mother gave me ten rupees a day to attend college. She said she had no income. Terrible liar. Her new source was funding plenty of McDowell's whisky. That ten rupees was supposed to pay for the bus fare, the newspaper, which I could not do without, tea and a snack. I never stepped into a bus. I mean, who was she kidding? I was used to aeroplanes. I got more money for an outing when I was at the boarding school. My meagre pocket money was the primary reason I avoided going to college. I walked to and fro, and avoided snacks and tea to save the money for magazines. One day, a girl I had only seen but never met or spoken to in college said *Ami tomake bhalobhashi*, I love you, to me. *Teri toh!* That song instantly played aloud inside my head. I was wearing a lemon-yellow shirt. Or was it a vermillion-red shirt? Vanity had not yet become pride. I had not even looked at myself in a mirror like that! Boarding school had surely made me internalize my femininity. Was the quietude in its place projecting my masculinity? My voice, my gait, my mannerisms were changing. I was a different person from the one I knew in school, where every move I made was observed, scrutinized, criticized. No one was calling me a girl, a sissy, a chhakka in college. And now a girl was proposing. What? It was so random. Could she not see I was a naazuk boy? Was it because she did not know me? Was it because I was no longer in a jail-like restricted environment? Was it because I was no longer doing those singing-dancing things I loved? I had, of course, outgrown them, reflective of the kotha's unmusical environment now, but did that make me a lesser naazuk boy?

A Christian fellow who lived in an adjacent gully started speaking to me in the street. It was unusual, but I enjoyed the attention. Once, he said he would like to take me to the Bow Barracks to meet a friend who was great at giving a blowjob. Blow jaw? What is that? I asked. Blow jaw like a blow to the jaw? I had misheard. I was not familiar with the term. 'Blowjob' was not listed in the Oxford dictionary. (This was the Nineties. I was soon going to find out in-depth about blowjobs after reading *The Starr Report.*) The chap nodded. Why would I want a blow to my jaw? I asked. Arre, it's nothing like that, man. It's a fun thing to do, he said. Just come, na. I was on my way to college, so I thought a little detour would not upset my routine. Bow Barracks was two minutes' walking distance from Bandook Gully. We walked into a shabby slum-like corridor. An effeminate young man opened a door and said to come back later. He had a guest. I was relieved. I felt something suspicious and shady, so I decided never to meet them again. The effeminate guy's feminine appearance, wearing what looked like a woman's blouse, a loose sarong, long hair and faint make-up made me nervous. I recognized part of me in that person, but the other parts of me resented it. I was not like them. I did not want to dress or look or talk like that. I was called sissy, a girl, but I did not look the part. I did not want to be one. Was this me looking at myself in the future? What if I became friends with this effeminate person and hung out with them? I would become them. I was a timid character in the streets, keeping my head down and walking as far away from the crowds as possible. I did not detest the safety the kotha offered. There were fewer men inside to bully and tease me, depending on the hour of the sun. But this was different. A seemingly jovial, harmless-looking fellow was sweet-talking me into something that could get me in trouble, had I been successfully lured into it and begun seeking it independently. I could not let a person from outside the kotha try to take advantage of me sexually. What if word spread? What if they blackmailed? What if word reached my mother? Or the young boys in the mohalla? It would be a repeat scenario of my ordeal at the boarding school.

Vicky had made friends with the boys in the Barracks. He played football with them in a field outside. It was dangerous to flirt with him, but he knew how to keep a secret. He had more than his fair share. I invited him to watch late-night television with me when Mother was away. He was a great kisser. We slept together. He was so gentle in bed. I felt I was finally going to have a lover of my own. When he saw me in the street, we did not talk. I knew then that he was not telling the Bow Barracks boys about me. We managed to hook up one more time. He went to Kerala for a vacation. I never saw him again.

My Aptech pal Nikhil encouraged me to go on a date with a girl he vaguely knew from his girlfriend's college. He had not figured out my orientation. I had, but it was not the right time to tell anyone. I met the girl in an ice-cream shop in New Market in the morning. We quietly licked our favourite flavoured scoops—hers chocolate, mine vanilla. We made small talk, smiled uncomfortably, exchanged phone numbers and left. Later, that girl sent me a love letter written in blood ink. Mother found it. Is this blood? she asked. Goat blood, I said. What did I know? I was myself in shock. This girl was nuts. A tawaif's daughter in Sardar Ki Baari had previously sent me a few friendly letters, as did I. That pen-friendship ended abruptly when the letters stopped coming. I had a phone pal, a girl I had never met. I liked talking to girls, writing to them. It did not mean I was interested in them. I was not professing undying love and affection to them. Whatever they made of my friendliness was not my headache so long as they did not express it in blood. Kothari made the bloody letter a perfect excuse to convince Mother to send me to Poona. That will teach him how to be a man first, he said. Posh diktat from a man who had abandoned his wife and child somewhere in Jodhpur. I could foresee him doing the same to Mother within a year or two. But who was I to tell her? She was on his side. A three-way argument followed between us. Two, actually. I was the non-confrontational party. Mother locked herself in the kitchen, saying she will immolate herself. I was getting out of hand. I thought of running away. I thought of suicide. My suicide, not hers. I knew she would not do anything rash to harm herself. She wanted to play the victim, but her life had made her too fierce, too scarred, to ever truly be one. Even my thoughts of suicide lacked the conviction to act. I was also never a victim. Like mother, like son. Life always seemed too beautiful to ruin it when I looked up at the old, rusty ceiling fan whirring above my head in the room where I was confined, as if the fan would fall on my head to hug me with its three-armed blades if it found out about my plans.

I had seen Mother fight with my father. She had poured kerosene on herself. She was fidgeting with a matchbox. I was peeping from a quilt. The loud sounds of their quarrelling voices are muted in my recall. Neighbours rushed in and saved the day. My father took me to his own house in Macchua Bazar. His wife and children stared at me. *Mere dost ka beta hai*, he said to them. My friend's son. He told them his friend had a domestic situation at home. I doubt his wife smelt through his whisky- and cigarette-heavy breath. I involuntarily became a vault for my father's secrets and lies. I played with the fat white rabbits in a cage in their house. His wife fed me a tall glass of warm milk with almond flakes in it. They were all dressed in white. Like their house was the Kaaba. They waited for me to sleep before he could explain to her what my name was. I was back with my mother the next morning. That brief episode in my father's house has an afterlife, an all-white dream quality, like a homeless child being assigned a new family in heaven after committing suicide.

I went to live with my maternal aunts in Poona, returning once a year to Calcutta for my college exams. I was not interested in attending classes. I was a socially awkward teenager. I did not speak the local Bengali language; I could not relate to the teens my age and could not make new friends. My orientation disoriented me further. I went to Bhat Nagar in Pimpri to shed my naazukness. The abandonment of self-consciousness, the shedding of shame, gave me a more rounded character in the slum. I met Gora Mausi. She was tall, had a broad frame, a manly gait and a loud, quarrelsome voice. Her brittle, brown whiskers could have earned her a spot as a foul-mouthed sarpanch. She had never been to school, abandoned her husband right after marriage, did not have children, smoked, drank and gambled like a pesky crow in a window. The one thing she could have done to add more colour to her Amazonian personality was twirl her moustache. I was intimidated by her, but secretly admired her outspokenness. Everyone called her gaandi—mad woman—in pede ki bhasha, or the Kanjar dialect they spoke.

Mother occasionally called to check on me at a local STD booth. One time she called and said, *Tujhe college mein prize mila hai.* You have been awarded a prize at college. *Kis liye?* What for, I asked. For not attending college? No, she said, you topped the class in English. They sent me an invitation. What! Earlier, this lousy college used to fail me in English. I told her to attend the felicitation ceremony. She felt proud to receive the award. I had graduated. Later, she called to inform me the prize was a book. Which book? I asked. *Pataa nahi, ab mujhe padhna thodi aata hai,* she said. I don't know. I can't read in English. She chuckled. *Par sunn*, she said, *papa line pe hain. Baat kar.* But listen, your father is on the line. Speak to him. *Kiske papa?* I shot back, puzzled. Whose father? *Tere, aur kiske?* Yours, whose else? she confirmed. An awkward silence followed. My father said hello on the conference call of the pre-Zoom era.

Hello, I said. *Aap kaise hain?* How are you?

*Theek hain,* he said. He is fine.

*Aapke bachche kaise hain?* I asked. As if it was the most natural thing to politely ask a stranger about their kids' well-being.

*Kya matlab aap ke bachche—kya tu unka bachcha nahi hai?* My mother jumped in. What do you mean his kids—aren't you his child?

I fell silent. An accusatory silence we all understood as his neglect. It became clear that none of us thought alike. Like the distant call, the two of them were apart from each other, and me. Even a small whisper, meant to draw us closer in this intimate space, could widen the gulf with its acuity.

# The Noughties

I HAD BEEN LIVING IN THE SLUM FOR TWO YEARS WHEN MOTHER CAME to see me. Kothari had left her. She brought the book I had won in college. It was Plato's *Republic*. Some books come to you at the right age, I suppose. Plato's dialogue made me a philosopher! The allegory of the cave made me think of the slum—its dwellers as prisoners of their own shadows, unwilling to grasp a world outside, which I had known since my release as a prisoner from the boarding school, but right now I, too, was momentarily trapped in the fallacy that the slum was my best hope. I had come here to tell the poor that they could have a better future, but they would have none of it, content in ignorance. It was I who had to get out.

Meanwhile, Mother took me to a village to meet an underage girl, who served us tea. I understood she was trying to fix a bride for me. I was nineteen! My time to escape was near.

The community will accept us if you marry in the jaati, community, she said.

I think Mother had been excommunicated from the jaati because she had not returned to it after her sham child marriage. I did not care about the jaati. I did not understand it. All I saw around me was poverty and a lack of sanitation and education, worsened by rampant fornication. When Gora Mausi heard about my mother's plans to fix my engagement, she scolded her. Can't you see how naazuk your son is? Was she berating Mother with her own word—naazuk? Did she understand? Did she know? Gora Mausi's tone was enough to set my mother back. Naazuk, she had said, defining that age when one is beginning to metamorphose from teenage to adulthood. I was not a man but a confused boy. She had observed me. I did not show any obvious signs of being queer, but my interest in books, my low voice, my general demeanour as a non-aggressive person was at odds with the active boys in the compound. She reckoned that there was more to my sensitive nature than just these attributes. Did it spring from Gora Mausi's own anxieties of being different? She was an unusual character who did not fit in.

I now think of Gora Mausi as Josefa Ruiz Blasco, the aunt of the painter Pablo Picasso, whom he painted in the *Portrait of Aunt Pepa*. In 1896, when Picasso was fifteen, he was summoned by his uncle Salvador to sketch a picture of one of his aunts, Josefa. She was a spinster, characterized by her foul moods and extreme religiosity. She did not like the attention and fussed about being immortalized in a painting. It shows, if somewhat unflatteringly, with remarkable virtuosity in the painting. Some of the qualities resemble Gora Mausi, or all aunts who defy the standard. Picasso was nineteen when his aunt died. I was nineteen when I last met my aunt. There are no parallels between Picasso and me, but if I were to draw one, I did, back then, capture an image of my aunt's immortality in my mind, and only now attempt to paint her final portrait in words. Maybe Gora Mausi was queer. Maybe her lack of femininity was a way of channelling her rebellion, just as my naazukness was something I was trying to overcome by asserting my sexuality privately to the violence it attracted.

In my time in Bhat Nagar, I was making and selling desi daaru for five rupees a glass in Shanna Mausi's house. Was this how my future looked? It was fun in the beginning, learning how to store tin cans of rotting molasses with baking soda under the earth to ferment, and then later distilling the vile-smelling slush in a process called Bhatti, where it is poured into a drum, covered with a lid holding water that bubbles, and the alcohol collected in drops in a glass bottle connected to a rubber pipe plugged into the drum.

It was not fun when the police came visiting. They rounded up my aunts, cousins, relatives and neighbours who sold weed, in a van, leaving me out because one of them said, *Isko mat daalo, yeh yahan ka nahi lagtaa.* Don't put him in the van, he does not look from around here. Was I supposed to be flattered that I did not look poor like my cousins? I was offended that they did not see me fit to experience a night in lock-up. I gathered it would be a great story to tell in my future flourishing career as a celebrated writer who could drop such gems without a fuss, chuckling and not playing a victim of fate.

It was a proper check, fun moment aside—what was I going to make of my life?

My cousins were trying to teach me how to ride a bicycle. They laughed that I was too old to start. I agreed as I fell off the cycle. Another cousin tried teaching me how to ride his autorickshaw. I successfully turtled it, emerging unscathed in the accident. I found the only library in Pimpri Chowk and read some pulpy novels, comics, magazines—anything this small city was reading. Tripe such as *Men Are from Mars, Women Are from Venus* and *The Celestine Prophecy*. I cannot even recollect what these were about, despite the obvious Judgement Day titles.

I began looking for a job. A proper desk job, unlike the petty, odd jobs in the slum. One of my cousin brothers in Ambernath took me to a hotel to apply for a cleaner's job. I inspected a room, was told how to change sheets and arrange pillows. It was nothing new to me. Boarding school had prepared me to make my bed every morning. But now, the horror of turning that privileged education was going to be wasted on a bellboy's job? Visions fused haphazardly in my mind, swinging between my past and showing me a bleak future ahead.

I spotted an ad to apply for a medical transcriptionist's job in a newspaper. I did not know what it meant. All I understood from the ad is that the qualification was for an English-proficient candidate. It was either this or my cousin would soon fix my bellboy posting in that Ambernath hotel.

I went to the Deepak Nitrite office in Yerawada and sat for the aptitude test. I was an Arts student bunking college, and here I was, trying to bluff my way into my mother's dream of me becoming a doctor. They hired me, saying I had scored more than some science applicants. How was that possible? They were looking for candidates with basic grammar and spelling skills. I had read a decent number of books. That helped. They trained me with others for two months. I was decent in transcribing a doctor's audio notes into text. After two months they asked me to sign a contract saying I would not leave—bonus was dangled to lure. I panicked. I did not want to be tied to a chair. I became confident that I did not have to rely on my mother's family for work either.

I sat in an autorickshaw in Yerawada, ruminating about my future, when a ladybird glided in and sat on my arm. I saw it as a sign to take off. We took off home. I returned to Calcutta.

Having no one at home in the kotha to guide me, I did not know where to start. There was no precedence to follow. No one from the kotha had a salaried job outside. Whom could I ask?

One of my mother's old patrons, Banwari Babu, asked me to sit in his shop in Badabazar. His owned a wholesale cloth material store inside a congested lane. I did not return to it after two days. I found the work beneath my intellect, bowing to and servicing customers demanding to pull out this swatch and that swatch of fabric bolts from the shelves all day. I found another salesman's job in a retail store showcasing ready-made denimwear of a reputed fashion brand. I brought my bad luck to the store. The owner mysteriously shut the store in less than a week. I worked as a salesman for a car wax polish. I did not sell a single box.

Yet again I scoured the newspapers to apply. An advertisement in *The Telegraph* brought me to the Oberoi Grand hotel. My dream was going to come true. A pretty lady conducted a group interview. She was looking to hire telecallers for a loyalty club membership programme. I was rejected due to my lack of confidence when I did not answer promptly. I was nervous, sitting in the hall of affluent aspirants. I looked out of place and out of my depth here. I smiled nervously and befriended a girl sitting beside me. We exchanged numbers. I called her a week later. She said the loyalty programme was looking for admin staff. I met a man who hired me on the spot. Both these jobs, the one in Yerawada and now in Calcutta, were because I was reading a newspaper every day, looking desperately. Reading made all the difference. The first assignment at Oberoi was tough. I had to deliver the loyalty membership package to a milkman in a cowshed some fifty kilometres from the city. I nearly fell into a mountain of shit. The milkman offered no fresh cream of thought or salve if I had fallen deep. Another time I was sent to a tannery. I ran out after delivering the document. The stench in the place curdled my tummy. A vomit volcano reached my mouth. The manager was testing my naazukness. He thought I would not last a week. I lasted the entire six months the programme ran. I was hired as a runner. I was told to wear a tie. To tuck my shirt in. To shave. To comb. I found an unopened and unused bottle of Calvin Klein's Eternity perfume in my mother's almirah. It became my signature fragrance at work, where the telecallers said it made me smell sexy in the rains.

Phullo began gossiping in the kotha that I was working as a toilet cleaner at the hotel. Mother did not have to prepare tiffin for me because I was now eating lunch at the Oberoi. Tea was at the Oberoi. Sometimes even dinner. I was so posh. We went to the nightclub Tantra. My manager lent me his dinner jacket for an art show. I memorized the spelling before sipping Beaujolais Nouveau red wine. I looked at art like a curious bird, trying to outline the face of Jennifer Lopez in an abstract figure. The blackboard advertising the day's specials in the restaurant included millet flatbread. Reading it made my worlds collide—Bhat Nagar, where I used to eat bajre ki roti every day, and here I was, about to nibble on it as a unique speciality food in a five-star hotel. No one had asked me for my background before I joined work. My ability to speak in English was sufficient. No one knew my home address led to a kotha. Between the bourgeoisie, the bordello and the bread, I could tell no one where I went after office hours. The world had no need for it here. It was a meagre salary, but gave my confidence the boost it needed. When the programme rolled up, I got a job next door. The S.S. Hogg Market building opposite the Oberoi housed a Citibank call centre on its topmost floor. One of the telecaller girls at the hotel, Bipasha, was kind enough to recommend me for the job. Her boyfriend worked there. I was hired on the spot because I spoke English without a Bengali accent. I was trained as a telephone executive. The salary was better. It was Valentine's Day when I got there. I got a rose from a girl and thought I was special. Mother thought I would become a banker, if not a doctor, as she had desired—still a more stable job than what was about to happen. Buaji, who worked for us at the kotha, came to the office daily to deliver a tiffin box. Mother sent food like I was a child in school now. A fat, bespectacled colleague was surprised to see the quality of our food. Oh, so you eat gobindobhog rice, fancy ya, he said, commenting on the moderately expensive grain in an inconspicuous stainless-steel dabba. That was the first time I realized how class-conscious people were. I had to be careful. Everything was judged. I did not know my mother's favourite small-grain gulab swaroop was called gobindobhog in Bengali. There was so much to learn, apart from work, at the office.

I spent my weekends borrowing books from the British Council library. I bought and tried to read Sigmund Freud's *The Interpretation of Dreams*, although I mostly slept sound and dreamless, and mainly identified as a daydreamer. This book confused me more than Linda Goodman as she doled out hope in her astrology books. More than a year went by at the call centre without me making a single friend, but instead straightening my spine, sitting upright all day and modulating my voice to sound less naazuk. Then ennui set in. I despised telling Bengalis who called repeatedly all day to check the balance in their account. As if it was looted in their afternoon naptime nightmare. I drew doodles all day. I started thinking about my life ahead, now that I was making my own decisions. What about love? What about sex? I was accidentally, but now curiously, checking porn in a cyber-café cubicle. Was this what my life was going to be? Static? Buffering? I wanted out. I wanted to live alone, be free, have friends, drink wine, watch movies and read books. It was not possible at the kotha.

Ajay, Phullo's son, saw me accompanying my mother's patron Dilip Sir to the Bowbazar tramline. I was helping the old man with a cane and a limp into a tram. Ajay said I made a good pimp. No matter which station I was in life, our kind, the sons of the kotha, who had not achieved anything on their own merit, always pulled me down. The allegory of the cave shrouded the kotha.

I started applying for jobs outside Calcutta and looked at options in Delhi and Gurgaon, where General Electric was setting up back offices. I secretly applied for a post. I went for the interview held at a hotel in Calcutta. Which is the last book you read, the interviewer asked. Franz Kafka's *The Metamorphosis*, I said, with the confidence of a liar. I had not read it. I wanted to. I had only read a graphic version of it in the magazine *Gentleman*. I got the job.

I returned home and played the songs of *Devdas* on full volume. One final time to make the kotha feel its former glory. I did not dance to *Maar Daala*. Allah! My heart wore ghungroos. This went on for nearly a month. I would return home from my job at Citibank and blast the music. *Bandh kar!* Mother yelled, irritated. Shut it! *Naak mein dum kar diya, kotha bana rakha hai*, she laughed. What a nuisance, turning home into a kotha. She was right. A kotha could be her home, but was it ever mine?

On an uneventful day in April 2002, I boarded a train from Howrah to Delhi. I only remember the colour of our clothes. I was wearing an indigo-blue kurta with white pyjamas. Mother was wearing a red sari, her favourite colour. She stood on the platform, sobbing and waving goodbye. I think she may have been feeling the first pangs of a life-long separation. I felt nothing. I had told her I was never coming back. I did not know I was being selfish, unkind. She had no one but me. I was breaking her heart forever. There was nothing to come back to this city for. Not even for her. We were not friends. We were just mother and son. A formal relationship being casually shrugged off. As the wheels rolled with a hiss and a hiccup, I turned from the door to walk towards my seat, abandoning her like everyone else who had come before me.

# Seventeen Years Later

# 2019

At sunset, I arrive at my mother's flat in Calcutta. It is Christmas Eve. I am carrying plum cake and macaroons from Nahoum's. There is a blunt red transparent plastic knife in the cake box that may have to be replaced with a real one. Some cakes break knives. The plum cake will soften her belly and melt her stolid heart. Hopefully. I ring the bell. An alarmingly loud chirping-sparrow sound makes me laugh. I am reminded why I am back here. Jesus!

She opens the door.

Surprise! Merry Christmas! I say.

She shows no surprise. The candle is blowing hard in the stolid wind. She tries to smile. The best time to corner her is on a religious occasion. Propriety sobers her. I wish I had brought a bottle of Shiraz. We could do with some cheer. Her vibes are never agreeable. I could say it is Jesus's juice. She would buy that. Not on any other day, but today.

Drinking with her son in a shareef mohalla! Oh dear! What will people say? *Christmas mein toh sab peete hain.* Everyone drinks on Christmas. She has used that excuse before. I leave after she distributes the cake in cheap, faded plastic plates with a green leaf print. She sends it to ten apartments in the building as 'Kirismaas ka prasad'. Christmas offering. Rum balls from Flury's deck the plates. All her neighbours are book-abiding Muslims. Alcohol is haraam. The inquisitive neighbours will gobble up the haraam balls and plum cake, desperate for a second slice of my life. Why am I back? This is my second visit this year. A record. The previous year was my first in six years. Before that, memory eludes us all.

The previous year, how can I forget, we had a mini showdown. I heard her speaking to a Singhji on her phone. I do not know who he was. She was telling him about me. *Pataa nahi kyon aaya hai, muft ki roti todh raha hai.* Don't know why he is here, breaking free bread. I confronted her. Who is he? She flared up. Who are you to ask? It turned into a screaming match, by the end of which she was provoking me to hit her like my cousins in the Poona slum did, raising their hands on their parents. According to her warped logic, that is how parent–child roles reversed. Disgruntled by her outburst, I said violence did not run in my veins. I left.

In another attempt to reconcile, seven months ago, after my rent lease agreement expired in Bombay, I stowed away my books (including my recent birthday gifts Michael Ondaatje's *Warlight* and Bruno Munari's *Design as Art*), my only wealth in a friend's house, and came to Calcutta to see my mother on her pretend birthday. A birthday we had made up for her some two decades ago. She did not know when she was born. I wanted her to have a date like mine. Our birth dates are separated by a little over a month. Mine in April. Hers in May. Four years ago, she stopped calling to wish me on my birthday. I asked her how she could forget. *Mujhe lagaa tujhe meri zaroorat nahi hai,* she said. I thought you no longer needed me.

Every time she said something so convoluted, I went speechless. What could I say to that? It had its own special chime in my heart, to the sound of eternal damnation. I could either sulk that she forgot mine or celebrate her birthday, which she was born without.

We should write your story now, I had said. *Kaun padhega*? she had replied. Who will read it? I had played the audio version of my *Arré* essay from the previous year, which had gone viral. It had Neena Gupta interviewing me, and was translated into a Hindi audio story. Mother looked like she was warming up. To sway her, I told her a story.

This is the following anecdote, but without the flab.

In 2005, Neena Gupta and Soni Razdan were jogging on Juhu beach. Nothing unusual about it. A routine run. Then something happened. A dream rose and sank like the waves. Did they notice? I was standing ankle-deep in the water, watching the sunset, when I spotted them. What was I doing at the beach? Pondering, as usual, whether I should quit my day job at a back-end office in Vikhroli to pursue writing. I thought I should approach the ladies and tell them to inform Mahesh Bhatt that I had arrived. I *had* arrived! That is it. No permission to interrupt their exercise routine. Just announce. The two women, busy chatting, jogged past me, glowing in the yellow light of the setting sun. I imagined their reaction for a moment, narrating to Mr Bhatt the clown they had met at the beach.

Neena: What a pompous ass he was!

Soni: Strange, no? What does he mean, tell Bhatt Saab I have arrived. Who the hell was that moron?

Bhatt Saab: Must be a dreamer. Everyone is coming here, but who is really arriving? I think it is the golden hour that turns dreams to shimmery dust.

Indeed.

My dreams were returning to a dull, brown shade in the wave's ebb. I wanted to be a writer Mr Bhatt would hire for a film. I had nothing to show. Where had I arrived if I had nothing to declare? It was a decisive moment, watching the two ladies jog ahead. I was a nobody. I quit my job. I returned to Bangalore, where I worked previously. Lived in a hovel. Consumed copious amounts of literature, music and cinema. This was my routine for three years. In a diary, I recorded those years as: *Life has subsisted my daily ration with such meagre allowance of luxury that I take small breaths in this room. I am not scared that if I take a deeper, fuller breath the room will open at its seams. It's a room so compact in design and hermetic in appeal, I can't think big; living in isolation of feeling, breathing with less hope, surviving in fair dealing.*

It now sounds like I was torturing myself to become a writer. I was going to be terrible at it if I continued to write like a certain Russian novelist. I felt confident and returned to Bombay in 2008 after a singer I met at Koshy's told me he believed my blog was a sign that I should go. Really? The blog had rancid poems that could make a cat retch. I was hustling two jobs at the time. I had a day job as a content writer and I helped my friend Abhishek on the weekends, organizing queer parties in pubs.

I left Bangalore. I reached Bombay, struggled for a month to find a decent place to live in, got lucky soon and locked myself in a room and wrote a film script. Now what? Was I ready? Hah! I walked past YRF Studio every day. It was close to where I lived. A film-maker who was struggling as an assistant read the script and said it was perhaps the best script I had written, but that I should rewrite it after ten years. How was it the best when it was the only one? I was a novice. I heeded his advice and put the script in cold storage. Cut to ten years later, my first novel was out. In 2019 Neena Gupta was interviewing me for the Audible story. Me, that pompous ass from the beach! I told her about how she had inspired me. She chuckled.

Dreams ebb and flow.

Mother listens to a shorter version of this story without expression. I tell her how a literary agent has got in touch after reading the essay. I have written a proposal. An auction among top publishers has led to a book deal. *Humari nilaami hui hai*, I tell her. There has been an auction for us. She chuckles at the irony. I cannot tell if she is convinced. I will have to check another day.

When the leftover Kirismaas cake has dried up in the new fridge, partially eaten, I ask if she has thought about narrating her story. There is no expression on her face. She cannot afford Botox. It is just her resting bitch face from a hundred years of isolation. When will she crack? I hope she dies with a smile.

*Ghutno mein dard hai, peeth mein dard hai.* She complains of weak knees and a bad back. Her time is coming. Life has not been kind to her. She makes it a point to drum it into me every opportunity she is not given. I will have to sing along to her tunes, following her wobbly sur. Her consternation reminds me often of the poem *Sorrow* by D.H. Lawrence. It is something I have long dreaded that I will have to enact like a scene on a stage play.

*Ah, you will understand;*
*When I carried my mother downstairs,*
*A few times only, at the beginning*
*Of her soft-foot malady …*

So much drama! I get weak knees just thinking about the scene.

I meet a photographer and his social worker friend. They walk me through the filthy gullies of Bowbazar where sex work is the main attraction. It is a subject for the photographer and a noble calling for the social worker. What am I doing here? I did not ask for the tour. They just decided they want to show me the real Calcutta. I begin despairing for the women to be working in such appalling, unsanitary conditions. I grimace all through the tour. As we waddle through narrow lanes covered in dirt, edifices shaky, toilets dank and dirty, and a bazar of noxious scents assaulting our nostrils,

I ask my guide if these quarters were once the balakhana, kotha, for mujras. She says that is unlikely—only sex work thrives here. So I say there must be someone here who wants to sing and dance. She says I am being a tourist. Oh well! I stop walking. I hear a sound. An answered prayer reveals itself above my head, from the leaky tenements we are crossing. It is the rhythm of ghungroos tied to a girl's unshackled feet. Can you hear that? I ask her to stop and listen. She does. The music stops. She walks. The rhythm picks up where it left off, and walks with me. The girl is practising. Or is it me hearing the muffled sounds of my unbidden past? The universe is transmitting a musical message.

In the evening we head to a writer's X-mas house party. I carry a bottle of wine. Another world-famous-but-not-in-his-country writer is at the party. I have read his books. I like the chatty women in his novels. They have a queer vibe, which I can pick is his own motormouth persona. I introduce myself. His girlfriend hangs on his arm like a carelessly draped shawl in this nippy weather. The famed writer says, I read your essay about your mother working as a prostitute. Awkwardly I smile and say, Tawaif. A world-famous writer cannot get it right—how will anyone else? I am not upset. Just amused. I am used to this mix-up between sex work and nautch work. Anyone else would have probably smashed cake (not the rum variety on the table) on the writer's smug (and loud) face. I find a corner to nurse my freshly made mulled wine. That is two of us mulling. It feels urgent for Mother to tell her story.

# 2020

*YEH SIRF APNI CHHATI HILA RAHI HAI,* MOTHER SAYS.

As crude as it sounds in Hindi, there is no better way of saying it in English. Translating it to 'she is just shaking her bosom' is romantic poetry compared to the raunch that the Hindi word 'chhati' implies.

She is watching Sapna Choudhary jiggle her breasts to the Haryanvi words *Manne pal pal pal pal yaad teri tadpawe se* on YouTube. Sapna is dancing on a makeshift stage in the Ullawas village in Gurgaon. She is dressed in a fitted navy-blue knee-length kurta and a hot pink Patiala salwar. Sapna dances with the enthusiasm of a gymnast, shaking her hands and legs vigorously, as if warming up to perform an impossible stunt. She is lip-syncing to a man's throaty voice. It blends perfectly with her somewhat mechanical moves, marked by an aggression that the unruly crowd of raucous men are enjoying. There is nothing in her performance to suggest the adaaigi, coquetry, nazakat, elegance, shokhii, playfulness, or tehzeeb, etiquette, associated with being a tawaif.

Mother makes a gesture of disapproval—her chin shooting up sideways—as if she is crossing out Sapna from her dance class with a slash mark in a checkbox: Disqualified. Mother does not own a dance academy, but has the confidence of a masterji. A masterji like Saroj Khan, perhaps. My mother is no match for the curvy Sapna Chaudhary, but the curiosity in her eyes, the discipline in her attentive moves could get her a TikTok fan base if she knew what people do for fame these days. Sapna is an acolyte to her. Mother immediately puts her right leg in front, balancing her bony body on the balls of her left leg, ankle up. She drags her feet forward in perfect sync with her hands, swaying like an octopus in a swimming contest. This is how we used to do it, she says. Her flailing arms synchronizing with her feet remind me that I have seen her do this step thirty years ago. It rushes to me in the smile of a ten-year-old child. How she danced to survive. If life was an ocean's currents, she was the luminous octopus rhythmically swimming against its tides. Graceful, but also sad to watch—the same move slowed down by the wear and tear of several years of living in her own shadow. She puts a hand on her hip. Harappa's dancing girl. Mother is wearing a fitted but worn-out maroon kurta in which her breasts have flattened. She probably weighs as much as a sack of chicken feathers now. She catches her breath in the dusty Belgian glass mirror on the wall—a bright yellow gold-framed time machine with a fading lacquer finish that no longer reflects the brilliant lustre of her heyday. The wrinkles on her forehead and the crow's feet around her eyes have crumpled her moon face. Time's needle has crocheted her into a different woman. I am beginning to look like my mother, she says. Don't we all? There is a dull sheen on her face from the quiet years of living alone, immersed in prayer and longing.

Her hair is thinning. She colours the greys to a jet black. Her pupils are paling into grey stones. Her vision is fading. Her mouth is always red, thanks to the gutka she chews. She has switched to inferior brands. BABA zarda and Natraj paan masala cost more. She claims she cannot afford them. Her financial net worth belies her. Her fixed deposits run into several lakhs now. Her savings are unheard of for a woman who never learnt to count. *Padhi likhi nahi hoon, na*, she says. *Par paisa sab ko samajh mein aata hai.* I am not educated, but everyone understands money. This will not be the first time she will mention her parsimonious triumph over her illiteracy. I have tried telling her that she should splurge on herself.

Look after yourself, I have been repeating with futility. Her smile has been wrecked by years of addiction to cheap tobacco and betel nuts. *Iske bina pressure nahi aata*, she says. She reveals a set of chipped, irregular teeth and her dependence on gutka for her bowel cleansing. I look at her and parse words in my brain. She used to be so beautiful. Time ravages everything to pity. Or a child grows up.

I have never cared for her. She will not let me. Or anybody else. She is a tougher nut than the areca she snaps with a silver sarota. *Aye, Simmi, chai dekh zara*, she says. Oi, Simmi, check on the tea. Simmi is stirring tea in the kitchen. Simmi is a young girl with small features, a tall frame and a stammer that makes her invisible to people. Simmi checks on her once a day, fetching aloo-puri for breakfast and gossip for chai. She is rewarded with gutka. Simmi cannot function without the nasha, Mother snitches on the young girl's addiction to gutka. Simmi lives in a tin-roof room shabbily built on the terrace of the same building where Mother lives on the first floor. Simmi lives with her father, mother, sisters and brothers, who are salesmen in a garments shop. It is a family of ten or more in one room. She is unmarried and looking. Families reject her for her stammer and her crooked posture—she has a limp. That has never stopped her from dreaming. She fetches the best scrunchies and hairpins from the market for her hair makeovers. Simmi also spends most of her day sitting by the roadside tap, filling water into jerry cans and chatting with the shopkeepers. It makes her look disreputable, but she is in a hurry to wed anyone who comes forth for a sip.

Simmi enters the room with tea and breakfast. She cannot hold the plate straight. It slants. Breakfast is not elaborate. The aloo curry is bland and the puris are flaky. The bitter black tea makes me retch. Don't you drink milk tea? I ask my mother. *Kaali chai. Doodh kaun la ke dega?* Black tea. Who's going to go get milk? she says.

I can smell thrift in her tone. She saves, or rather stocks up, for doomsday.

*Sirf paisa kaam aata hai mushkil ghadi mein, log nahi.* Only money counts in hard times, not people, she reflects.

She is at home in her boxy, ochre-yellow bedroom. The mirror covers an entire wall, an artefact of significance where nothing else is. There is a twenty-inch flat-screen television on another wall—a new addition.

Which brand is it? I ask.

Samson, she says.

That name is perfectly clear to those familiar with the Samsung brand. I do not correct her. She calls the Nokia brand 'Konia'. Initially, it took me a while to follow her unique language, but I was quick to nod, chuckle and move on.

A low-lying bed covers half of the tiny room, lined with bolsters—in the style of the gaddi where the raees, patrons, sit and watch the mujra. The decor is a remnant of the erstwhile kothas. She has had one bedroom ceiling painted to reflect glowing stars in the dark. *Chanda ko dhoondne sabhi taare nikal pade*, goes the lullaby she sang for me. She had hoped I would come and stay with her. Those unhappy stars seek this moonface.

She lives in an unpainted, grey three-storey building, where she proudly claims to be the only Hindu resident in a Muslim ghetto. She is, of course, making a point about religious intolerance in the country. She says she hates the place but that she also loves it too much to leave. It sounds fairly confusing, but she is now a creature of irrevocable habit.

*Sab aise hi hain.* All of them are the same, she says. Her chin goes up again to disqualify no one in particular. *Kahaan jaayein?* Where else to go?

I realize that the dismissive chin dance is a defined dance step in the Hindi-film universe from the Sixties, where the hero is trying to woo the petulant heroine in a rose garden. The heroine usually accompanies it with a 'hmmph' and a comical twist of her painted red mouth—all the more arousing to her suitor.

Mother's apartment smells of hot cooking oil and the shitty smell of a gutter that runs on one side of the building under her window, sending up gases so rank that it is not possible for me to spend a day in her flat. I try to do my business as quickly as possible if I have to use her toilet, never quite sure if I am adding to the foul scents. It is an Indian-style toilet. My nemesis. I have not sat on my haunches in twenty years.

I am getting familiar with her new environment. It has almost been two decades since I left the kotha for a call centre job in Gurgaon. She had to leave the kotha ten years ago. She moved into this flat when the landlord paid her fifty thousand rupees for the eviction. The mujra business was over. The patrons had moved to discos, dance bars and brothel rooms with air conditioners. When tawaifs were being ushered into dimly lit bars where they were asked to sway to Bollywood tunes for the rheumy eyes of lecherous men, what did they do?

The existing dance bars in central Calcutta are the desi version of strip clubs, except that women there do not have to wear next to nothing. In some of the illicit Bombay dance bars that began to proliferate in the Eighties, the women stripped down to nothing, as seen in Mira Nair's 1985 documentary *India Cabaret*. In the years since, the dance bars have been raided and the women have gone sanskari. Indian men prefer a fully draped woman to a naked lady. They want to be the ones to undress her. Men's hot, glaring eyes peel off the clothes of fully clad women. That is inordinately sexier than a woman who bares all and leaves nothing to the imagination. In dance bars, women are displayed as easy playthings, artless whores who prefer this form of listless shimmying to begging on the streets. Even the daily-wage labourers who huddle at the crack of dawn await the construction manager, who will pick them for a specialized skill set. What skill do these swinging women bobbing their bleached hair have to offer? Fuckability? A question a tawaif probably asked herself when entering this new space was: What am I doing in a dance bar? I don't sing here, I don't dance (I swoon like a retiring pendulum in a rusty clock tower, where my time is ticking), I don't have a band of musicians to await my taan for a thumri. I don't have to serve paan with bashful eyes and coquettishly adjust a disobedient pallu. Money is showered on me for nothing I do here. I stand and stare at the blank canvas of my future in this bar. Why should I be paid for nothing? Have I no value? Can I not earn it through performance? Is standing here more respectful than standing on the streets? I can sing, I can dance, I can flirt, tease and engage in a meaningful conversation. What use is my adaaigi if I cannot employ it as my craft? This isn't my fiefdom at all. I am not advertising my talent. I have a show to put up somewhere else. Where is the gentleman patron who appreciates me? They are swigging beer in a crowded caveman's den and hooting like a baboon. The tawaif feels like a talentless Barbie doll in a dance bar. When the tawaif sang *Salaam-e-ishq meri jaan, zara qubool kar lo* in a kotha, every man sitting in the audience believed it was meant for him and him alone. *Tum hum se pyaar karne ki zara si bhool kar lo*. The courtesans sold adaa, and the men read the second line as a prompt to romance them—but it did not permit them to overstep.

What my mother saw in the dance bars could never be agreeable to her. The women were groped, fondled; they entertained men by sitting on their laps. She could never consider it an option because it felt unsafe and dangerous to her. She had seen her cousin sister Hasina perform in a dance bar. It felt dirty, cheap and vulgar, compared to the safe space of a kotha. *Woh kala thodi hai, bas sirf aise-aise hilne mein,* she says. That's not art, just shaking from side to side.

I decide to step out on to the balcony of her apartment. The view from there is alarming. A sulphurous urinal, a garbage dump, a hair salon and a charcoal-fumed restaurant for daily-wage labourers operate under it.

On one side of the narrow lane, skinny young boys are yelling at a carrom match. A waspish girl sits at a water tap, filling cans and bottles, murmuring to herself. A mangy dog yelps in the rubbish when poked by another. A stringy cat lounges on the tin shed above the urinal, in the shade of a neem tree. A loudspeaker hangs on a branch to announce the call for prayers at a mosque.

This is an environment alien to me. The one before this did not seem as much.

The kotha was a music box that remained a sturdy block of wood until opened. Once you entered it through the innocuous main gate, you were removed from roz-marre ki zindagi, the drudgery of the daily, ordinary life. Roz-marre ki zindagi is a favourite expression of the toiling working class. I have picked it up from my mother, who has wizened with it—a philosophy to keep moving underlines its quotidian usage.

The kotha was ensconced in its own magical universe. That world of kathak and ghazals and mogra and the cackle of women after an evening of song and dance; eating meals together, exchanging stories and storing hard cash in rusty almirahs in the tenement, keys dangling on a challa on their hips, hooked to their petticoat, bindis leaving their foreheads to be pasted on smoky mirrors, like a dot on a calendar marking their attendance in full glory.

Mother now lives in what she has constantly reminded me over the years is a shareef mohalla. A respectable locality.

*Koi nahi jaanta yahaan,* she says. No one here knows.

Who is she fooling? Everyone knows something.

I wrote several articles about you on the internet, I say.

*Computer pe?* On a computer?

I have to break it down to her in simple words.

Ekta Kapoor was interested in making a serial about you. A producer from her production house called me to discuss the story.

*Phir?* Then?

I said no.

She draws a blank, stops chewing.

*Kyon?* Why?

I have to remind her that Ekta's serials are loud. I do not want them to do that dhain-dhain. I try to produce the jarring music with a chin dance that television actors are forced to do on the editing table. She likes some of Ekta's serials, at least the first few episodes. She admits she was hooked to the new one about a djinn before it became repetitive.

That's why, I say.

I tell her that it is important to document her story because the culture of kothas and tawaifs is over.

Look what has become of it now, I say, reminding her of the dirty dances on the internet. She perks up and wants to discuss Sapna's bland moves. Sapna could be a modern-day tawaif—a version alien to the old form, but somewhat connected. Sapna is trying to conduct herself with dignity on stage, both in her choice of fully covered costumes and her dance moves—not too far off the mark with the lost and forgotten tawaifs, who were cut from the same sequinned cloth.

Sapna is the most famous face of the disco mujra in the country. Men go crazy when she slides a hand over her bosom to the lyrics *Tera roop jigar ma radh ke aag lagawe se.* My mother would have been too embarrassed to thrust her bosom, or even touch it in her time. *Humare time mein gracephool tha.* We had more grace, she says, pronouncing 'ful' as 'phool', fragrant as a bud. Her conceit, anachronistic, is well intentioned. She only wants to preserve her era in a bubble of decency.

In professor Veena Talwar Oldenburg's widely read and cited essay published in 1990 about courtesans, 'Lifestyle as Resistance: The Case of the Courtesans of Lucknow, India', she writes about the tawaif's opinions about their status and morality in the 1970s.

> Those who dare to hold 'moral' objections to the life of a tawa'if should first examine the thankless toil of an average housewife, including her obligation to satisfy a sometimes faithless or alcoholic or violent husband for the sake of a meagre living. Such an existence is without dignity, and was not the situation of the housewife tantamount to that of a common prostitute, giving her body for money?[1]

Talwar Oldendurg echoes the sentiments of the courtesans who point out to her how they are in a better place than housewives.

---

1. Veena Talwar Oldenburg, 'Lifestyle as Resistance: The Case of the Courtesans of Lucknow, India', *Feminist Studies*, Vol. 16, No. 2, Speaking for Others/Speaking for Self: Women of Color (Summer, 1990), pp. 259–87, https://www.jstor.org/stable/3177850

> It is we who are brought up to live in sharafat [genteel respectability], with control over our bodies and our money, and they who suffer the degradation reserved for lowly [neech] women.

My mother, now vastly removed from present-day stage performances, sees Sapna taking over with raunchy dance moves and even worse music. It is degradation from her time, when the tawaif conducted her performance with nazakat. Going further back in time, even before the colonial era, when they were patronized by the royals, the courtesans of Lucknow would pretty much say the same about the Seventies' open tawaifs, who diluted the form by performing in large, crowded fairs, like my mother.

Sapna's ownership of her open-space mujra is in contrast to the traditional, old-style tawaif's close and intimate gathering of a select, private audience in a kotha. Mother will accept Sapna's popularity with disdain, because it means that she has to change as well to keep up with the times. If she does not, she fades along with what remains of the kotha. And it is here that Sapna fortuitously gives it a Shakespearean setting in a Haryanvi village: All the world's a stage.

I begin recording Mother on my phone.

*I do not know when I was born. Even my parents would not know if you asked them. But they have been dead for a long time. I never got a chance to ask them.*

*My being born was not an event. I was born at night, in a ramshackle hut on the outskirts of Poona. The tin hut was situated on a barren, dusty stretch on the side of a highway. On the other side were green fields. Fields as fertile as dreams we had never seen. In our homes, children are born like litter, one right after another. And in the cold night, if one dies of neglect, there is no time to grieve.*

Mother punctures her past with the present when she adds: *Which means I don't have a birth certificate to prove my citizenship in this country any more.* She laughs and makes a comment about our current government insisting on stripping us of our nationality if we do not have a birth certificate. She does not have hers. She did not collect mine when she rushed out of Lohia Hospital in Calcutta with me in her arms. That makes me an illegal citizen too. Her self-effacing style comes through with this sudden injection of humour into our conversation about her life, which she normally considers not worth talking about. It is evident that she is updated on the politics of the country. She swears by the television channel Aaj Tak. Aaj Tak is not good, switch to NDTV, I say. Listen to Ravish Kumar. *Mere cable mein nahi hai.* It's not included in my cable plan, she says. *Aaj kal sirf Aaj Tak chalta hai.* These days only Aaj Tak plays. Our small chat about propaganda TV is postponed.

As she recounts her life, the thorny episodes of her surprise wedding, the night of consummation, are awkward, particularly because it comes so immediately in her memory. She talks about it in a resigned tone: *Aur phir shaadi ho gayi.* And then I got married. As if that is the fateful quashing of every girl's dreams. No horizon beyond a married life. It is true for most girls even today.

What happened on your wedding night? I ask.

What about it?

Her pupils enlarge. She is prickled by the thought that I might ask for a detailed account of the time she, all of seven or eight then, was wedded. It must have been a horrible night. I am aware that I cannot continue this story without knowing my boundaries. Our mother–son relationship is not a rosy one. There is a deep ravine between us that this story can fill. She feels as if everyone has misunderstood her. This is an opportunity for me to make her feel otherwise. So I skip asking. If I rewind into my memory box, I can recreate what she went through. We were once watching the film *Bandit Queen* on television. There is a crucial, brutal scene of the child bride Phoolan Devi screaming and resisting her husband's forceful sexual advances. The loud background score stifles the little girl's piercing cries. I saw my mother choking back her tears, trying to overcome her emotions. The scene brought back something she had been trying to bury inside her forever.

*Yeh dekha nahi jaata.* I can't watch this, she said.

She did not change the channel. There was no avoiding it. She wiped her tears and continued watching the film as if she was fine with watching her life unfold. Survivors have an in-built remote for immunity that automatically switches on in the event of hardships. I watched her, but did not comfort her. I could have held her hand or hugged her. My reflexes as a teenager were like hers—to move on without seeking warmth. I wish now that I were not so much like her. Our suffering alone can make us cold, if not bitter. We do not respond well to love. We are capable of loving, but not showing love. I understand why she would not like to revisit that incident again. I already had an answer to that question. Perhaps she tried to raise her voice when she saw the molestation scene of Meena Kumari in *Phool Aur Pathar*.

*Madarchod! Maaro na usko!* Motherfucker! Somebody thrash him! she had shouted.

*Aye, sssh!* Babbo, her elder sister had said. *Yeh film hai.* This is a film.

*Woh kya hai?* What is that? she had asked.

*Jo hum dekh rahe hain woh asal mein nahi hai.* What we are seeing is not real, her sister had said.

This moment encapsulates the innocence of my mother's age. When her own husband was raping her, she probably thought this could not be real, that this could not be happening to her. She must have been in shock, frozen in fright and unable to defend herself, weak in body, resisting in mind, submitting in force. Did she think she was in a film? Like Meena Kumari. Helpless. I can never know what she went through. She was too young to understand what it meant. She was herded like cattle into a new domesticity. She probably thought it was part of her design, every girl's kismet, to be used like that. It was her duty to obey and resist revolt. What other choice could she have had? She did not know where she belonged. Where could she have run away?

*I was in Ramdas's house until I was twelve or thirteen, I think. I can't be sure, you see, I am not educated. I did not keep track of time, and memory eludes me.*

Mother has a tendency to associate her diminishing memory with her illiteracy. It helps her skilfully blur the details of her age. She will then throw a spanner in the works.

Ramdas is dead. Her husband. The one she got thrashed by a goon named Bhagwan Dada. Isn't the goon's God name just divine for vengeance?

I am shocked by this sudden revelation.

How do you know? I ask.

She has not seen Ramdas in nearly five decades. He was, in any case, a dead man to her from the beginning.

His sister, Cheenu, lives here in Bowbazar. *Milti hai kabhi kabhi.* She meets me sometimes, she says.

This news is my introduction to her husband, his family, his relatives—people I have never heard or seen before in my life. She has been very faithful to her secrets—except one time when she got sentimental about her struggles, recording herself on an audio tape.

Do you still have the tapes you recorded? I ask her now.

*Na, phenk diya.* No, I threw them away, she says.

Why?

Who keeps piling up all that rubbish? It went out as garbage with the other stuff when I left the kotha.

She could have made my work easier, but no.

We move on to discussing how she was nearly sold to a brothel. I feel it is important to ask her about sex, for no embarrassing reason, primarily to check how frank she is about it. *Pehle toh yeh sun, tab mujhe pataa hi nahi tha sex kya hota hai, mujra kya hota hai.* I must tell you, she interrupts, at that time, I did not understand what sex work was or even what mujra was. *Main padhi likhi nahi thi, na.* You see, I was not educated.

I am successful at not rolling my eyes at this point. My mother's lifelong tirade against her life has been based on the fact that she did not receive a formal education. She could have been someone worthy, she thinks. It is so deeply embedded in her conscience, interlinked with her sense of self, that it is worrying how it has begun to manifest itself in her old age. She blazed through her youth on the steely wings of her optimism. Not any more.

A particular recall rattles me.

*When he tried to feed me a rasgulla, I began to weep. I could not control my tears any more. I was also hungry. So I took a bite with relish. That bite might have satiated a great many hungers within me. The hunger of an artiste is to feed the imagination of the always-hungry audience. The opposite was happening here. Lal Saab's kindness was filling me up.*

When she narrates this incident about her dancing on an empty stomach, it brings a lump to my throat. It is a poignant and sad moment. She weeps as she revisits it. Watching her sob, tears trickle down my cheeks too. It is an automatic reaction, I suppose. I force a smile to continue recording her voice on my phone. She draws her strength from this present moment now, seeing her son go soft. I stop recording. Later, regaining her composure, she interjects her story with a tiny bit of pride to shield her emotions.

*Ekyasi number khaali hua karta tha—meri wajah se mashoor hua.* The Ekyasi number kotha used to be empty, I made it popular.

She says it with such nonchalance that it does not register as a matter of pride to me. It sounds much more as a key detail she forgot to mention earlier. It has now entered the conversation as a dramatic arc of her wide-reaching fame and its after-effects.

She laughs a lot in describing her friend, the qawwala Mallika Aapa's room. Which man would not like to wait in such a museum of tits! It is a room that I have also encountered as a child, walking around the four walls, looking up at the arched portraits with ample bosoms on display. A Felliniesque buffet. It was perhaps my own first introduction to unbridled youthful sexuality, at odds with the woman I saw before me in the room—a paan-chewing, whisky-drinking lady wrapped in a cream cotton sari, no inch of her skin exposed to remind one of her famous days. Mallika Aapa had auburn hair, a wide smile and the rheumy eyes of impending doom. I never heard her sing. She had stopped singing.

Which also reminds me, I may have got a faint glimpse of seeing my mother do her famous step of bending over to pick up notes with her mouth. A contortionist, like the girl in *The Exorcist* descending the stairs like a spider. As Mother narrates her move, I am reminded of a little girl walking on a tightrope, balancing a stick in her hand at a street corner—a common sight, in which a man usually plays a pungi and implores her with song to complete the task of walking from one end to the other. Crowds watch this impromptu circus act at busy street-light intersections, some even convinced to toss a coin for the intrepid performance. I imagine my mother as that dirty-haired, raggedly girl in a torn frock, amusing people to earn a meal. Does a tawaif feel the same way? Is Mother like a street busker? I have watched and marvelled at Meena Aunty's thali dance. Unlike gate crashers, kids at the kotha were a milder version of curtain wreckers. We were the first non-paying viewers peering into this world of bejewelled performers shimmering in sequinned saris and sweat. For us, these women were no less than circus performers. If they were the tamers in circuses, the patrons who came were the castrated lions. We watched the show for the patrons—the anaesthetized lions in joker clothes, the real clowns of the circus.

Mother's grim stories about the fate of her sisters Laccha, Rajjo, Laxmi and Hasina are in some ways different versions of herself. Some things that happened to them are some of the things she managed to dodge. She, perhaps, even saw them as cautionary tales. I remember Rajjo, Laxmi and, of course, the starry-eyed Hasina. In my adolescence, I spent a month in Hasina's Chandivali house. I was on vacation. She took me to film studios, hill stations, restaurants and parks. I got a taste of her high life, which, in retrospect, was a B-grade-movie life sponsored by a patron. A lifestyle that Mother could have enjoyed, but perniciously avoided. Several years later, I watched the 1983 Merchant–Ivory documentary *The Courtesans of Bombay*. I suspected Hasina Mausi was on the DVD cover. I showed my mother the film. She confirmed it was indeed Hasina. Where were you, I asked, when the film was made? I could see the kotha where we had lived once, but could not spot Mother in the film. *Yeh humara kamra tha.* This was our room. She points it out. Actors Zohra Sehgal spices pickles and Saeed Jaffrey smells a rose, speaking in glowing terms about the courtesans and the mujras. *Main shayad tab Kalkatta aayi thi.* I must have been in Calcutta then, says Mother. The film-makers had concocted all sorts of spurious stories in the film—one involving an alleged love triangle between my mother, Hasina and a local young man. Is this true? I ask my mother. *Sab bakwas hai.* It's rubbish, she shot back. *Main kyon kisi lafangey ke peeche padungi?* Why would I entertain a good-for-nothing? It was too late to confirm with Hasina Mausi. She was dead. I found a review of the film on the internet. American film editor and critic Glenn Erickson wrote:

> With its music and dance performances *The Courtesans of Bombay* would be a stunning documentary if it distinguished between authentic material and staged content. Even though there may literally be no difference, we have to trust the filmmakers [sic] as to the accuracy employed. The Merchant–Ivory team has a reputation beyond reproach, but doubts are raised by obvious staged content such as two courtesans sneaking messages to a shared boyfriend.

That settled it for me then. Especially Erickson's indisputable credentials as a film expert. He has worked as technical crew on two Steven Spielberg movies, if that helps to cement his authenticity.

But also, there is so much that Mother says that sounds incredulous. I know for sure she is not lying about it. I have heard versions of her stories, from her, her sisters and her nieces, ever since I was a child. I am only now putting it together and, as I give it a somewhat coherent shape, a perspective naturally forms: So many unbelievable things have happened to her that it does feel overwhelming at times. That should not strip it of her honesty, her truth and, while she is only getting this one chance to say it all, will she lie to her only child? She has nothing to hide, protect or hold sacred. She will no doubt leave out intimate details, she will not have proof to back her claims, she will not have a chronology, an almanack of records or paperwork, not even photographs (actually, she does have a few). It is only going to be an oral telling of her story—like the time she recorded it on tape. Every time I slide the phone close to her to record her voice, she looks at it with the earnestness of a suspect sitting across a lie detector, fully cooperating, or, even better, thinking of it like a radio interview—the kind that she is so fond of listening to as film stars relive their histories.

An instrument that unites Mother and me in our jobs is the radio. We have both grown up with it. Her day begins with switching it on in the morning, playing it all day like background music in the documentary of her life. Radio presenter Ameen Sayani's name popping up in our conversations connects us in more ways than one. Working as an entertainment reporter in Bombay, I had once telephoned his office for a quote on remixes. His stentorian voice—particularly his phrase 'Behno aur bhaiyyon', sisters and brothers, an early acknowledgement of our female listeners—must have been one of those accidental or carefully orchestrated wordplays that hypnotized fans such as my mother. His voice had recently been mixed with a Bappi Lahiri disco number from the Nineties for the 2017 Bollywood film *Badrinath Ki Dulhania*. His lackey told me he had no comments about it. I would have been just as awestruck had he used that famous 'Behno aur bhaiyyon' phrase to me when I persisted for an interview. My mother had passed on her radio craze to me. I grew up alternating between disco hits and sitting attentively for Sayani's *Binaca Geetmala* broadcast, like it was a voice booming from heaven. In yet another of director Mira Nair's films *Salaam Bombay!*, a memorable sequence shows a little girl, Manju, dancing to the melody of *Mera Naam Chin Chin Choo* when a radio announcer broadcasts it. Actor Anita Kanwar, who essays the role of a sex worker named Rekha in Kamathipura, is the little girl's mother. That sequence could very well have been a moment from our own lives when we lived there. My mother, Rekha, tunes in to the radio and jives with me in our small room in Bandook Gully.

Our radio has a quaint history as well. Phullo smashed it. She charged at it with a baton she had procured from a policeman. She said the radio was disturbing her sleep. One winter morning, Mother was cleaning utensils in the dalaan. I put the radio out on the charpai and played it on normal volume. Suddenly Phullo opened her door. She would watch cable television all night and only then would she be able to sleep when the light broke at dawn. My mother did not notice Phullo march out. Nor did I. I was sitting close to the radio. With the morning rays behind her, her shadow engulfed me as I watched a demoness straight out of *Amar Chitra Katha* pound the radio. My mother calmly got up and said nothing. We went to the satta don Rashid's house near Lalbazar. Mother spoke quietly, gracefully explaining her ordeal. *Mere bachche ko lag jaati toh?* What if my child had got hurt? she said, asking Rashid, Phullo's rakhi brother, to protect us from her violence.

Phullo's name retches up some horrible visuals. I saw her goondi side as well. Phullo, what a name! Like a daaku, a dacoit, hiding in the ravines. She made life hell for everyone. She would quarrel with the tawaifs all the time. It gave her pleasure to be the centre of attention when her dhanda, business, was dwindling. She lost loyal patrons because of her obsession with playing cards and gambling, and then, to make up for the loss, she would chase away patrons coming to see the mujra of the other tawaifs. She was despicable in every way. I watched her fight with my mother. The two women pulled each other's hair, slapped, scratched and screamed at each other. I stood frozen. Life had also taught my mother to settle her scores with fistfights. She was not very good at it, but it did not stop her from charging into the boxing ring. Phullo taunted Mother with being barren. Mother felt insulted and wanted to prove Phullo wrong. I think of the irony of this scenario. The tawaifs were desperate to prove they were childbearing women, even when there was no family or home they could provide for the child. Did they think this decision through? They were mostly pleased at the arrival of a girl child, but a boy could just as quickly turn into a menace. The boys grew up humiliated and ashamed of their origins. They could not contribute to the kotha or to their mothers' well-being without losing their own dignity. Which son goes out into the world to speak of his courtesan mother, when, right from birth, the world never forgets to remind him on a daily basis that he is a man, macho and all, and there is no place for a macho man inside the kotha?

My years at the kotha were the opposite of macho. Maybe I thought the best thing in life was to be a tawaif. Films reinforced the idea. Meenakshi Seshadri was a tawaif. Jaya Prada was a tawaif. Rati Agnihotri was a tawaif. Salma Agha was a tawaif. If such beautiful, gorgeous women could be tawaifs, what was wrong if my mother was the same, or me? The constructs of masculinity did not trouble me when everyone around me was losing their minds calling me names. If I sang and danced like a girl, so what? My speciality was mastering Shiva's dancing pose when the song *Hey Nataraj* played on the radio—a harmony of the yin and the yang. Not once did my mother tease or taunt me, or ask me to man up. I think that made all the difference. Had she said something to that effect, who knows what I might have become? Bad parenting more often ruins children. My birth was both a challenge and a gift to her.

*Khair, tu toh Khwaja Baba ki daen hai,* Mother says, referring to the saint of Ajmer, as if I were born of immaculate conception, completely bypassing the science of sex and discounting Khan Saab's tiny contribution to my existence. What if she had aborted the foetus? What if I was stillborn? Or worse? Like the time she talks about Tillo, the tawaif who was pregnant when she was killed by the goon Rab.

Did she have any other children? I ask.

*Haan, ek raees se tha.* Yes, she had a son from a previous patron *Woh ladka ab Dilli mein rehta hai. Gay hai.* The boy now lives in Delhi. He is gay. *Hormone ki gadbadi ho gayi, theek se ilaaj hota to theek ho jaata.* There was something wrong with his hormones. Had he been treated properly, he would have gotten better.

This comes as a total jolt to me. What is she saying? *Theek ho jaata?* Gotten better? But there is nothing wrong with being gay, I say. It is natural. She chooses not to react. She knows, but will not confirm. About me. I have, for years now, been hinting at it, telling her in not those exact words but circumambulating it like a Sufi saint. *Mera beta toh sant hai.* My son is a saint, I have sometimes found her saying to relatives and neighbours prying about my impending marriage. *Woh shaadi nahi karega,* she says. He won't get married. She has a deadpan expression. *Ussi se poocho.* Ask him, she says, when someone asks why not.

One afternoon, I insist that my mother take me to meet Afsar Aapa. Afsar Aapa was a courtesan several decades ago. She lives in Lalbazar. The building is called Chowdhury Ki Baadi. It could collapse any moment the wind decides to sneeze in its armpit. The Bowbazar tramline leading towards Lalbazar is where the kothas are. Building No. 269, Building No. 81, Sattawandi, Ramkali Ki Baadi, Sardar Ki Baadi—these were some of the kothas that have now been replaced by small businesses or low-income families. Aapa is holed up in a storeroom. Her children live in the main, big room. Aapa's rat hole has a creaky bed. She sits there all day, chewing gutka and occasionally staring out of the balcony at the traffic below. She greets Mother with enthusiasm and appears to be a livewire, chatting with a house help to fetch a Thums Up.

Can you tell me something about this kotha? I ask Afsar Aapa.

*Ab toh kuch nahi raha,* she says. There's nothing left to tell.

I was expecting this answer. I should not have asked. A retelling usually starts with this line: Nothing is left any more. I will have to be patient if I want to hear more. We excuse ourselves after small talk.

I will come some other time, I say. I know I won't.

When we step out, Mother says, *Dekha, inn se toh accha hi jee rahe hain hum.* See, I am at least living a better life than this.

She took me to meet Afsar Aapa because she wanted me to see the pitiable state in which courtesans languish. I acknowledge that.

I would like to meet my father, I say.

*Kyon? Kya zaroorat hai?* Why? Why do you need to meet him?

Has he never inquired about me in all these years?

*Haan, kuch saal pehle Rizwan Mama ne bataya tha unke ladke tere baare mein pooch rahe thay.* Yes, a few years ago Rizwan Mama, his relative, called me and said his sons were asking about you.

Why?

*Tere papa buddhe ho gaye hain. Aur namaazi bhi,* she says dissonantly. Your father is old. And also devout.

Oh, so he wants to atone for his sins before he exits.

She laughs.

I am the son from my father's absence. He wants to be present for me now.

Rizwan Mama meets us in his Lalbazar office. He runs a local cable TV business and is a small-time politician, he says dejectedly, like it were the same thing as being a small-time crook.

Please tell him I would like to meet him as well, I say.

Sure, I will inform the family, he says.

A month goes by, and there is no word from Rizwan Mama. It has been more than thirty years since I last saw my father.

And to think that this man once had the gall to suggest to my mother that she name me Aurangzeb, as if he was the Shah Jahan of paternal love!

Many, many years later, when poet Nida Fazli died, and when I was working as a reporter, I was summoned to write a quick obit piece for Scroll.in.

Fazli's poem *Walid Ki Wafat Par* begins with the line *Tumhari qabr par main fatiha padhne nahi aaya*—I have not come to read a prayer on your grave—which he wrote for his deceased father, whose funeral he could not attend. It inspired me to write a poem for my father, whose funeral I will probably never be invited to attend.

It must have something to do with mourning those we do not see but seek. Fazli's father migrated to Pakistan after Independence. They never met thereafter. My father abandoned me right after I was born. I am sure he is alive now, but I do not know if he exists. He ceased to long ago. Fazli had no progeny to bereave him, and so he wrote for his father, *Tumhari qabr mein main dafan hoon, tum mujh mein zinda ho, kabhi fursat miley toh fatiha padhne chale aana.* I am buried in your grave, you live inside me, come and say a prayer for me if you find the time.

I suppose I am conveying a message to my estranged father through Fazli's death, who was once transmitting the message to me through his father's demise.

About sons paying for the sins of their fathers.

Several years ago, when I was only beginning to imagine life as a writer, it would have never occurred to me that one day I would be writing about Fazli. Alas, when he was dead.

But writing heals.

I am not even sure if news of my father will ever reach me. Even when I reacted to Fazli's entombing poem and wrote, *Zinda dil tab hoga, jab tum uth kar padh doge fatiha jaage huay ek laash ke liye.* Alive my heart will thence be when you shall arise and recite a requiem for the living dead.

In one of our recordings, Mother reveals that my father had once kidnapped me after an altercation with her and asked her for ransom, meeting her at the Victoria Memorial gardens and taking thirty thousand rupees in exchange. I am shocked. I did not have prior knowledge of this. She had protected me from it for so long. I should at least ask him to return that money now, with interest.

In February, when the famous yesteryears cabaret dancer Miss Shefali died, I asked my mother if she had ever met her.

*Haan, aksar.* Yes, often, she says. *She was also called the Helen of Bengal. Once, she was performing at the Great Eastern Hotel—or was it at the Oberoi Grand? I forget. Shefali was dancing to Western tunes. After the performance, I met her to congratulate her on the spectacular show. I was at the hotel with a few other bais. We had come with a patron to watch her perform. We also happened to know the musicians playing for her through our ustads. A musician introduced me to her, saying, She is also a great dancer. I became shy and looked down. Which form? she asked. Not this one, I said, laughing.* Humara alag style ka hai. *Ours is a different style. Shefali looked at me as if she understood what I was implying. She winked at me, asking, Is it better? Not as good as you, I said. She laughed and hugged me.*

In February end, Mother travels to Jaipur with a Muslim neighbour to attend the annual Urs festival in Ajmer. I call her. I tell her to be careful to travel only at noon. There is news coming in from Rajasthan that Muslims are being targeted amid rising communal tensions across the state. That the northeast Delhi riots between the pro- and anti-Citizenship Amendment Act (CAA) protesters that took place a few days ago had affected neighbouring states as well. I advise her to reach our khadim's house in Panni Gully close to the Dargah Sharif in Ajmer and stay in. Remember to wear your bindi in the bus and carry your ID, I tell her. She chuckles and replies, I do not carry any bindi. Maybe I will get some on the way. I imagine her as a lone, old lady, head covered in a dupatta, walking into a cosmetics store and asking for a packet of vermillion-coloured bindis. Choosing the brightest tint, wearing it and murmuring to herself, Hope this shade is the most noticeable and makes me safe. She gets the bindi. The bindi, an old joke says, is a Hindu woman's forehead recording. Those few hours, when she is travelling in a bus, turns me into a ball of nerves. I pray that the bindi gives her safe passage into a warm and embracing Muslim neighbourhood, where the Ganga–Jamuni tehzeeb is espoused without a fuss.

After Ajmer, Mother decides to visit her family in Poona. Two days after she lands in the Bhat Nagar slum in Pimpri, the Covid-19 lockdown is announced. Planes, trains and automobiles are stopped from plying.

Please return to Calcutta soon, I say. Find the next train and get back.

I will, she replies.

If you cannot, go to your younger sister Rohini's house in Waki. It will be better if you live in a remote village. The slum is going to be bad news soon.

Okay, I will do that, she says.

She will not do a thing. I know her. So I have to plant ideas in her head for her return. Her nephew Ravi is a rickshaw driver.

Tell Ravi to take you to Waki in his rickshaw.

His rickshaw is damaged, she says.

Indeed, when else but in a crisis! I remember her niece Bansuri, her younger sister Shanna's daughter, is a sweeper at the Pune Municipal Corporation.

Ask Bansuri to arrange transport, I say.

Oh no, na, baba. I will not step into a municipality van. It will be filled with worse diseases. Bhat Nagar is a better place than being dumped in a garbage truck, she retorts.

In no time, most of her relatives are taken away to work in quarantine facilities. Some are given vitamin pills; some are given volunteering jobs in hospitals. It is a crazy scene in Bhat Nagar. Everyone is a suspect, even though no one has caught the virus yet.

Some people come here with a gun and point it at our head. I always go for a check-up. They never take me with them, Mother says. She means the infrared thermometer is a gun. Drama coddles her bones.

I guess you have better immunity, I try to calm her. You anyway live on a diet of medicines every day. Maybe it is helping.

*Haan, sardi ki, khaasi ki, gas ki, pressure ki, sab ki dawaai time se leti hoon.* I take all my cough, cold, gas and blood pressure medicines on time.

I am no stranger to Bhat Nagar. I was seventeen when I travelled to Poona alone from Calcutta. I asked a rickshaw driver at the Poona station to take me to Bhat Nagar. Our Kanjar samaj relatives had informed me that Bhat Nagar was the most famous place in the city. I assumed it was a great place to live in.

The rickshaw driver stared at me and asked, *Aap ko udhar kyon jaana hai? Aap toh padhe likhe lagte ho.* Why do you want to go there? You look educated.

I think of my mother as at least educated in that sense. She looks the part, whatever that means loosely, but not so in Bhat Nagar. Anyone can tell just by looking at her. Being stuck in a slum during the pandemic is reason enough to be worried about her health. She is sixtysomething, despite her false claims of being fiftysomething for a decade. She needs to get out of there.

My cousins work as security guards in a government bank and a government hospital in Poona. Some sweep roads for the local municipality. A few work in stores as salesmen. Most of my family members in Bhat Nagar make and sell illicit liquor and weed, and live recklessly, if somewhat harmoniously with the absolute filth and squalour. Bhat Nagar is infested—overwhelmingly and puke-inducingly—with filth. A flower bud could not grow there without being compromised. I went there as a wide-eyed teenager, wanting to see a world outside the kotha in Calcutta. Mother had sent me, saying her relatives would show me the good life. She put me in her younger sister Shanna's room. Shanna was married. She lived in the room with her husband, a daughter, two teenage sons and one kid. How would I fit into that room? When my cousins heard that I was educated, they informed me that I was the only one in their jaati who had gotten that far in school. They expected me to speak to them in English to impress them, but would they understand what I was saying? I refrained from any pomp and show because I had landed from the stars into a gutter, reversing

Wilde's quote: We are all in the gutter, but some of us are looking at the stars.

They treated me like an entitled prince or a foreigner. They expected me to spend money on them, and show them the rich and affluent life of the English-speaking, city-bred cousin. What was such a good life all about? Eating in fancy restaurants, watching movies in cinema halls, smoking and drinking, and wasting time as a gadfly. All this seemed fine to my agreeable taste in self-actualization, but where was I to bathe and shit? I could see pigs running around with their interfering snouts. I asked a cousin the evening I reached there, feeling dirty from the two days of train smog and dust. They showed me a water tap in the centre of the slum's compound, where women gathered with steel and plastic pots to fill water. What about the loo? A cousin picked up a small water bucket and pointed me to a vast tract of barren land across the road.

What? I was in trouble. I wanted to leave.

The cousins fawned over me when I told them about my boarding school in Darjeeling. *Aap ne baraf dekha hai!* You have seen snow! They thought it was in Switzerland. Switzerland was a mood, like a Yash Chopra film. I tried spending my boarding school knowledge on the children and adults, advocating cleanliness, hygiene and education, but it fell on deaf ears. I tried teaching the kids to read and write. They forgot their lessons as soon as the hour was up. I took them to parks and public places, the zoo and the fairs, but they preferred only the cinema hall. Not one elderly soul believed things could be better if they made a small change to their lifestyle. Instead, I think I learnt not to take my entitled self so seriously. I was whiling away time, avoiding college, which, in comparison, was far duller. I needed to learn to loosen up. I was an uptight kid just released from a boarding school, like a prisoner on parole. I had come to Bhat Nagar like a non-religious missionary without a purpose, and here I was, learning precious lessons to balance my so-called better life with this life that I thought so unwholesomely did not fit in with my personality. I was so wrong. This kind of reckless abandon in life gave me character.

Now, sitting alone in my Calcutta apartment, I worry about my mother. She is diabetic and has high blood pressure. I call her every day and remind her that she is going to be fine if she takes all the necessary precautions.

Breathe from your gut, I tell her.

She is always complaining about how bad it is to be stuck in Bhat Nagar. She goes there once a year for a few days. This time it has become an imprisonment. I remind her to be happy. That is the only thing I have been telling her my entire life.

Look at me, I say. Have I ever come across as unhappy to you?

She has no answer. No rebuttal, for sure. She knows nothing about me. I look happy. I try. I think it is a trait I may have unconsciously picked up in Bhat Nagar. I remind her that the unhappiest places give us a greater reason to live, to survive it. Is it not how she has been? I now think about it and wonder how it may have been the only survival trick I learnt from the Bhat Nagar community.

And look at all those people who are so different from us, I tell Mother on the phone. Their communal laughter is a thing of imperishable beauty.

Right? I ask.

Hmm, she tries to soldier on.

She feels utter despair, I can tell, but whom can she tell? What can she do about it? She sobs and cries and longs for her own home. No one can help her get out of the slum. She is stuck. A month goes by without any sign of a rescue—or an airlift. Her sky has gone dark. She is restless. What is it that I can tell her that will keep her calm? What can I do about getting her back to Calcutta? Will it be better being isolated, living alone at this very crucial time, or being together with your family? I have not even told her what happened to me. I was on the lookout for an apartment to rent when I came to Calcutta to write. I was clear that I was not going to live in her house, because that would not give me space to detach from her, and I was not ready to have my freedom curtailed. A Chinese lady and an Italian man were vacating a flat in the city. I went to see them to collect the house keys. There was no reason to panic. They looked fine. I was following the news of the virus in China and Italy, but only thought of it as a minor nuisance, not likely to affect me so soon. I fell ill the next day. I tried to recollect if I had shaken hands with them or hugged them on their way out. Of course, no one wore masks in the early days of the virus. Who knew what was to be done?

One day it was a runny nose. The next day I lost my sense of smell and taste. Another day it was a red-hot fever. Then I could not breathe properly. Next came immense fatigue. What were these symptoms of? A week passed like this—all alone, dying every day and being reborn. I recovered from my symptoms without any care or medicine. I had not left the apartment. Living alone all my life had insulated me from seeking company or help. I was new here. I did not know anyone around. I began to use my convalescence to start writing.

I have only just begun to listen to the audio recordings of my mother, and now I have to find a way to get her back from the slum before it is too late. If she dies, it will be on me. I will not be able to attend her funeral. But there is also a part of me that believes my mother will not die without me beside her. She is quite stubborn. She will not choose such an unhappy ending.

I had never returned to Bhat Nagar after I left it as a teenager. I felt life there would not dignify my education. I had to be somebody. The unexamined lives of my cousins, their invisible presence—my privilege as a person with a boarding-school education constantly reminded me of the chasm between us. I saw the slum as abysmal, with no hope.

Right now the people of Bhat Nagar are together, they are watching over my mother and keeping her in good humour. But this is a luxury that the vast privilege of my education cannot guarantee.

Towards March end, *She*, the web series, is released on Netflix. It was written and produced by Imtiaz Ali. I was part of his writing team, along with two women—Anuja Gondhalekar and Divya Johry. We did the writing work back in 2018. It seems like a series to binge-watch in the times we are in—a perfect engagement. Critics are not pleased with it in their reviews. My landlady enjoys it. I pass on her message to Ali. Some consolation. It is not as if producers are suddenly calling me to write shows. Once in a while I get an opportunity to flesh out a story idea, or a bible, or even a full script. Some people pay; some disappear. The business is such that one cannot rely on it alone. How I got that screenwriting gig was pure luck.

My friend Anuja, who was in Ali's writing team, said he was looking for an additional writer. Apply, she said. I was jobless, having just quit Scroll.in, where I was an entertainment reporter. My debut novel, *Lean Days*, was out, but that was not an achievement in Versova. When I went to the open audition call in Aram Nagar for an additional writer, there were lots of aspirants. Over a dozen at a round table. Some screenwriters were legends in their own tall words. Public speaking scares me. I was the first to be asked to introduce myself, which I was praying to a non-existent superpower to not be so. That is how wicked God is. I quickly mumbled my intro as a journalist, hoping no one would ask further. Everyone stared at me for being dull. One distinguished gentleman called his script a baby and said, *Aap apna baby lao, hum apna baby layenge*, and we'll kill it. Pin-drop silence. Everyone went rat-a-tat about their screenwriting skills. Some even had Tarantino braggadocio.

I felt small in that room. Insignificant. I had carried my novel to the meeting, just in case. I hid it. Ali must have consulted with Anuja. She must have insisted on considering me, saying I was a journalist, which might come in handy because the script was going to be a real-world scenario and we might have to meet cops and conduct interviews. I was in. Ali briefed Anuja and I, shared the story, guided the screenplay and took us out to a fancy members' club, where the children of Bollywood stars swam in a pool in the afternoon while their mothers enjoyed a cool beer. We discussed the script over bhajiyas and chai. It was surreal, surrounded by Bollywood's first (or second) wives club. Ali never asked about my background. He did not know. He was the politest, coolest celeb I had met. We went over certain scenes. He was open to inputs. He listened to us and developed, at this point, if I may say so myself, a fine script. It took us about half a year to write it. Then the unit got bigger. Film-maker Avinash Das was one of the co-directors on the series. He had made the lovely *Anaarkali of Aarah* with Swara Bhasker. Ali told us not to visit the film sets. That was an even better idea. Film shoots are boring after the first hour.

In the film business, someone who connects Mother and me deeply is the actor Rishi Kapoor. Barely a month after the pandemic was announced, the actor died of leukaemia. It was a shock close on the heels of another greatly loved actor Irrfan Khan's death. I called my mother in Poona and told her that her favourite actor, Chintu—Rishi Kapoor's pet name—was no more. She observed an involuntary moment of silence, mourning perhaps her own sense of disconnectedness from Aaj Tak, having no access to a television since her entrapment in Bhat Nagar. She had seen Rishi Kapoor up close during the filming of the song sequence *Om Shanti Om* in the film *Karz*. She had jived along. *Meri umar ke naujawaanon*, he sang. *Dil na lagana, O deewano.* People of my age, do not recklessly give your heart away. She had been smitten. Here she was, really, an extra in the crowd, a young woman feeling fortunate enough to be in the same room as a privileged man, gawking at this charismatic third-generation superstar from one of India's most instantly recognizable film families and wondering if giving her son his name would be a sure-shot way of ensuring that a similar level of hysteria followed me everywhere.

She did not name me Rishi. She went for the character's razzle-dazzle. There were big block letters on stage that spelt M-O-N-T-Y. She must have asked someone what those letters meant. The name felt electric, or at least the disco lights around it gave her an out-of-body experience. She decided to give me the pet name, the ghar ka naam, daak naam, as they say in Bengal. It was misspelt as Montu on my birthday cake. Bakers tend to play truant with cursive writing on special occasions. The Montu cake was one kind of privilege I had even before I learnt to read and write.

In 2018, a friend, Surabhi, who worked as an assistant director, took me to a cast and crew screening of the film *102 Not Out*. The film featured the actors Rishi Kapoor and Amitabh Bachchan as two bickering old men making a lot of noise on how to live peacefully together. It was time to be overexcited and clap again like a child. But Rishi Kapoor was the child this time. His played his role like a grumpy child in the film. And he was an ebullient child after the film credits rolled. An easy way to manoeuvre your way to Rishi Kapoor in a crowded room is by listening to him speak. His commanding voice identifies him before you see him. He has the animated energy of a child. What were the chances that my mother and I, in different times and circumstances, would happen to be in a room with the same celebrity? Here I was, an extra in a crowd too—but I did not feel the rush of fortune like my mother. Rishi Kapoor's notoriety as an irritable man preceded him. I was not going to endanger myself by approaching him only to make a fool of myself. The occasion reminded me of how I rediscovered the terrific actor

I never really liked in *Luck by Chance*. In the film, he plays an old-school film producer risking his reputation by staking his money on a new talent, Farhan Akhtar. I could have walked up to Rishi Kapoor and said, My mother named me after your character Monty. Just as the tyro launched by the producer in *Luck by Chance* did. It would have made me sound childish, trying to steal the attention away from Rishi Kapoor. Or it would have launched my career as a writer under the illustrious (and defunct) RK banner that his multitalented father Raj Kapoor had founded. I stayed behind and watched Rishi Kapoor through his words dancing in the air. He was the star child in the room asking, Where is my favourite toy? His favourite toy was life itself—his vitality to have fun and play with it was a joy to watch. When I read the news of his hospitalization, I did think that he would not make it through the next day. Gloom shrouded the film industry. I woke up to a song playing outside my window. *Tu tu tu tu tu tara, phans gaya dil bechara*. The same dil that Rishi Kapoor sang about when my mother was in the room with him: *Dil na lagana, O deewano.* The same dil I was hearing of when he had left the building. Only he could make it cute and believable in the way he sang *Phans gaya dil bechara,* like a man-child in the film *Bol Radha Bol.*

When I tell my mother about the actor's death, she takes a moment and says, What else? I guess it was just a motherly way of avoiding morbidity between us in this climate of uncertainty.

Happy birthday, I say.

Thank you! You remembered? she says.

Yes. How are you going to celebrate it?

What to celebrate? I hate it here. No one cares for me. I survive on the rookhi-sookhi, meagre, meals I get.

Don't worry, you will be fine. You know how to look after yourself.

Hmm, I make the most of my rookhi-sookhi.

The choreographer Saroj Khan's death saddens my mother when she hears about that too from me. In Bhat Nagar, she has little or no access to a television, let alone a remote control. News reaches the slum late. When we speak on the phone, the conversation goes something like this:

*Aap ne suna? Saroj Khan guzar gayi.* Did you hear? Saroj Khan passed away.

*Oh, kab?* When?

*Aaj subah.* This morning.

*Arre, arre.*

*Aap toh mile bhi thay.* You had met her.

*Haan,* Patita (I hear patootie) *film ke set par.* On the *Patita* film set.

*Oh, woh dance kis ko sikha rahi thi?* Whom was she teaching dance to?

Shoma Anand.

*Bas ek baar miley thay?* You'd met her only once?

*Nahi, nahi, kai baar. Shanmukhananda Hall mein unka dance programme dekha.* No, no, many times. She performed several times at the Shanmukhananda Hall.

*Kabhi baat kiye?* Did you ever speak to her?

*Arre, nahi nahi. Hum log toh duur se dekh lete thay.* Oh no, we used to watch from afar.

She talks about the girls from the Congress House kotha who could not muster up the courage to speak to her because of their background as mujra performers.

*Par Bandook Gully mein toh sab khoob nachte thay Saroj Khan ke dance ki naqal kar ke—woh* Mere haathon mein nau nau choodiyan hain. But everyone in Bandook Gully used to dance to her numbers—such as *Mere haathon mein nau nau choodiyan hain.*

I used to emulate the nagin dance in *Main teri dushman* quite often.

*Haan, woh toh bahut chala. Par uss time tak hum log ko maloom nahi tha ke dance kisne sikhaya. Saroj Khan toh baad mein zyada popular hui, na.* Yes, that was popular at the time. But we did not know who choreographed it. Saroj Khan became famous much later.

*Kab?* When?

*Jab woh Madhuri ko sikhane lagi.* When she began choreographing for Madhuri.

The television boom of the Nineties made Saroj Khan a household name.

*Kaun se gaane pe?* Which song?

Dhak dhak karne laga. Dhak Dhak *toh bahut mashoor hua. Par woh mari kaise? Dhak Dhak* was quite popular. But how did she die?

Heart attack. The dhak dhak that made her famous also stopped her heart.

Mother is stuck in the slum for six months, distraught and drinking like a dehydrated fish in a filthy water tank. I call her every day to assuage her fears. I try to put her on a plane a few times, but she is not willing to travel alone. She says she will get lost at the airport. I imagine her on a flight to nowhere. When she finally boards a plane after a few cancellations, she is prepared for the worst in the pandemic—she is willing to endanger her life to get out of Bhat Nagar.

She is so frail and shaken; she falls ill the day after she arrives home in Calcutta. When I pick her up at the airport, I carry a sachet of her favourite paan masala, Vimal. She had told me on the phone that she could no longer find it in Bhat Nagar and that she had to rely on a local mixture of betel nut and lime powder. Poison. As television news anchor Arnab Goswami was screaming *Mujhe drug do, drug do, drug do* on his propaganda news channel, I was slyly slipping this narcotic paan masala into my mother's hand, coaxing her to take a phaankh, a mouthful, in the Uber ride back home.

But where will I spit? she asks.

Ah, roll down the window when you see an opportunity, I say.

She did what all good Indians do after deboarding an aircraft—she spat everywhere. The freedom is short-lived. Within three days of her return, her feet swell up. She complains of weakness and fatigue.

At home, she tells me many stories about the slum, but the one that cut the deepest is the story of Bansuri's son, Sujal. Bansuri is Shanna's daughter. The same Shanna she tried so hard to educate. Shanna died of breast cancer a few years ago. Bansuri's husband has also been dead for a long time. She is a municipality sanitation worker, having got the job that was once her husband's. Her teenage son, Sujal, is openly gay and unhappily accepted in the family, although the samaaj, the panchayat, has not yet taken cognisance of it.

*Woh galat raste pe chala gaya hai*, says Mother. He has ventured on the wrong path.

*Galat rasta?* Wrong path? I ask.

*Woh gay ho gaya hai*, she says, gesturing with her hand as if to indicate he took a bend in the road that led to a ditch. He has become gay.

Become gay? How does one become gay? Being gay suddenly feels like a Robert Frost poem. Alone, in the middle of nowhere, deciding to take the road less travelled. This is my mother, who otherwise thinks she has a liberal take on most things in life. How can she think being gay is taking the wrong path?

She has been telling me about the women in the Pimpri slum—how they had begun to take agency of their own bodies. How they slept with whomever they wanted to outside of their marriages. And no one was to blame. Then how could being gay in an environment like that be considered wrong? Do the women not support the gays? Is the slum also home to many marginalized communities?

The Dalits, the hijras, those from SC/ST? It seems the people in the slum tolerate it, but do not approve of it. Men need to be macho. Women are becoming fierce. The in-betweeners, the queers, need to either belong to the weaker section, such as the hijras, or correct themselves. I had lived there, I had seen and heard a few things, but it was not discussed back then. Sujal's acceptance as a gay person is not acceptable, but tolerable. That would not have been the circumstance twenty years ago. In my time there, my cousins had told me that when there was a wedding in the community, one room was used by young boys to fuck a chhakka, their word for a sissy boy. They would take turns at him. It was an unspoken custom. Sassily dressed girls thronged these weddings. Boys would drink and get horny. A sissy boy from the slum would be violated that night.

Does he have a say? I had asked my cousin.

What say? he asked. He is a sissy. He wants it, we give it.

I was shocked, unable to comprehend their savagery. During Bansuri's wedding, the cousins had indulged in this behaviour. And what if Sujal, Bansuri's first-born, also had to go through the same degrading, dehumanizing ritual when he grew up, as a teen?

Did I give off sissy vibes when I lived in Bhat Nagar? I was extremely self-conscious. I was manning up, or at least that is what I thought I was doing, correcting myself for the so-called sissy behaviour that I was ridiculed for in school. I was also reading a lot to shield myself from sporting activities. I borrowed cheap paperbacks from a library in the market, but I saw my reading as a distraction in this environment, where it was considered rich to waste time on books when there was so much activity around to indulge in—children fighting, murderous women screaming, drunk men talking to the wind, dancing moths, singing dogs, jumping pigs, shitting cows, sneezing horses, slutty cats, thieving crows, sergeant ducks, renegade goats and suicidal chickens. The slum was infested with chubby rats, giant cockroaches, sneaky spiders, angry lizards, strange fleas, venomous mosquitoes, even a scabby monkey or a dead bat swinging from a tree. Who would, then, have the time to read a book? This was nature, louder than words. Only a sissy type would read a book, but to even classify me as one, these people would have to go to my school to learn its definition first. Reading books protected me from accidentally displaying my sissiness, had the boys asked me to throw a ball or run across a field—typical giveaways of a gay boy not interested in sports.

Bhat Nagar was not only low on sanitation and hygiene, it was even lower on ethics and morals. The lines were clearly defined between heterosexual and homosexual. To be queer, one had to be a sissy. It was just the way it was seen. My mother's telling of Sujal's story is a slight improvement from my time at the slum. He is probably seen as a sissy, who has taken the wrong path of coming out, openly choosing to call himself gay.

Sujal's wrong path is all over his WhatsApp story feed. He posts pictures of emo boys in stylish haircuts looking sad and weepy. The videos he uploads are songs about tragic love. The young boy is named after a character from the television serial *Kahiin To Hoga*. He does not bear any likeness to the television actor, but his mother would have thought otherwise when she had decided to name him after her favourite soap opera character. I cannot overlook the irony of the serial's name *Kahiin To Hoga*, He Must Be Somewhere. What will happen to him as a young, gay man in Bhat Nagar? I must try to reach out to him and support him. Maybe my own courage will come from him. If he has been accepted, even if begrudgingly, will his wrong path not pave the way for me?

Mother suffers her second stroke. I do not even know she ever had a first. I only find out now that it had taken place a few years ago. She did not know what was happening to her then. She was alone at home. She was crawling on the floor to reach the bathroom, she told me later. This time she is paralysed on her right side, her speech is impaired and she almost dies of her comorbidities, including a seventy per cent failure of both her kidneys, fatally high blood pressure, diabetes and a persistent urinary infection affecting several other vital organs. I joke that the stroke should have struck her left side. She signs cheques with her right hand. I might need some cash for an emergency.

Actually, I do not even know clearly how much of her body is in working condition. For the next few days, I give her a bath, change her diapers, train her for potty, comb her hair and feed her chicken soup. I occasionally dance to a Helen number, *Iss Duniya Mein Jeena Ho Toh*, to elicit a smile from her immobile face. I accidentally become my mother's mother. She becomes the child I never wanted. I joke that soon I will have to breastfeed her if I put on any more pandemic weight. I am going bald up, she is going bald down. Okay, sorry, too much information. I call my friends and tell them I am lactating. My ovaries are ripe. I try to make light of the situation in the absence of having a friend in the city. The jokes are a coping mechanism. All this while the Covid virus is spreading venomously across the city, the country and the world at large.

In the Calcutta chapter of my first novel I had written about the city: One more day in living is one less day in dying. This is not only true for the city, but also for the times we are currently drowning in. There is death, despair and really no hope left. My mother is the only Hindu woman living alone in a four-storey building, where all the other tenants (over a hundred people) are Muslim. Everyone still calls her Rehana Aapa, informed by her past. The building is situated next to a mosque, which most men from the building visit for daily prayers. I cross the mosque every evening when I walk to my mother's house from my rented apartment, carrying her dinner, expecting her to look and feel better for one more day. This is my routine. It has made me come closer to death than anything in my own life. Luckily, no one in her building has gotten the virus since the lockdown. The virus will spread here like a forest fire when it does. My pulse races when I see people assemble for namaz, but months have gone by as I have watched them in silence, my mask shielding the horror on my face. I am constantly reminding my mother's friends and neighbours to mask up. Compared to the naked, mad sadhus jumping in hordes for a Ganga snan at the Kumbh Mela, flashing their filthy arses and stupidity, the namazis maintain distance for wazu, decorum, as they gather and perform their prayers without chaos. Compared to the evil politicians campaigning for votes, the Muslim community is at home, fasting and praying during Ramzan. I am not saying that they will not get the virus and not pass it on to my mother, but even my ailing mother could become the lone, Hindu, super spreader in the Muslim mohalla. No one is immune to suspicion. Not even me, an intruder in this environment.

My mother will not survive when the third stroke (or Covid) comes knocking. The only real job I have had in this pandemic is trying to keep her alive and cheerful. She wanly discusses the cost of electric- versus wood-cremation procedures. I show her yogic postures to reduce her flatulence. We accompany Asha–Lata songs on the radio and gossip about the skincare regime of retired film stars popping up on television after years of hibernation. I cannot resume working full-time as a film reporter because my mother refuses to adjust to fish-eating Bengali ayahs and chatty house help from Bihar. I hire two ayahs in two shifts. As Mother begins to recover from her slurry speech, she chases three ayahs away. I programme the fourth one to pretend that she is deaf. Mother chases her away. She can be quite territorial in her kitchen.

I have not been social—I have not made new friends. I am away from my peers in Bombay and now live alone in a Calcutta locality I am not familiar with since the pandemic began. My landlady, a doctor approaching senior status, is my drinking buddy when I go to her house to pay rent. I rely on sad memes, cat videos and female-led films to cope through the rest of my day when I am not thinking about my mother's unpredictable health. I no longer exist for my own dreams. If this is what it means to be a parent, I am glad I am only going to litter the world with baby-face (or Nick Jonas) emojis. It is tough trying to manage everything alone. I never ask for help. I realize that only recently. I am so stubbornly resilient that all it takes is an innocuous question to crack my brittle exterior when someone at the hospital, where I am a regular now with Mother, asks: Are you okay? No, I am not. Accepting I am not becomes the struggle to overcome and seek help. The clarity comes with the doubt of thinking, What use can I be to anyone? And not speaking up or reaching out to others in need of assistance. Being my mother's mother is my trial by fire with the barest minimum relief, but when it comes, rarely, in sputtering sparks, that joy is indescribable.

Mother's nephew Ravi calls me and tells me she had been drinking heavily in the slum during the pandemic. She was depressed. When she had come back to Calcutta, the doctor had told me seventy per cent of both her kidneys were damaged because she did not treat her diabetes for years. She could be put on dialysis any time now if she does not strictly follow the diet chart and medicines. Mother uses her molly sheets like a dastarkhan, tablecloth, for her fish curry and rice meals. She curses and hisses—her mood swings affect me more than her. She often takes the wrong medicine, despite my best precautions to keep them away from her. She behaves like the stubborn kid I never was. I walk her to the balcony, make her sit on a stool. She contemplates quietly, like a cat, looking up at the piece of the sky through the grills above her. The radio is on. I suppose she is waiting to hear *O Phirkiwaali, Kal Phir Aana*, like a final melody to wave goodbye. It is the first song she remembers learning the words of while still a little girl frolicking around the green fields of Poona with her favourite goat, Neelkamal.

Four days before Christmas, Mother calls me and says, *Mujhe kuch zaroori baat karni hai. Jaldi aao.* I have something urgent to discuss. Come quickly. I was getting dressed to go out for dinner. I had just sprayed YSL's M7, and was feeling confident and sexy in its woody-amber-whatever notes. And now I have to think that she is dying. I rush down the stairs, bolt through the main gate and run. I reach her house in twenty minutes, huffing and puffing. When she gets to the door, she has a calm expression.

What happened? I ask. She looks fine—if one can say that to a terminally ill patient, just to reassure oneself, rather than to prepare for the worst.

*Andar toh aao*, she says coldly. Come in first.

I follow her into her bedroom, which also doubles as her visiting room. She walks ahead, sits in her favourite spot and says, *Main jaldi marne waali hoon.* I am going to die soon.

I interrupt her before she can give me the big talk. I have seen this coming. I do not want to encourage it. I want to head out for dinner.

Maggi? I ask. Would you like Maggi noodles?

She nods. I slip into her tiny kitchen and boil water in a pan. I return, check her medicine box and try to distract her with general chatter about her neighbours, the hawkers under her window, her errand girl Simmi.

*Mere gharwaalon ka ek list banaa, jin jin ko main paisa dena chahti hoon.* I want you to make a list of the relatives I want to give my money to, she says.

Oh, okay, I say. Here's your evening snack. I hand over a bowl of soupy noodles. Sure, in time we will make that list, but first please eat your soup, I say. She slurps. I watch. Your sisters lived for very long, and so will you. As she finishes her snack, I hug her, kiss her forehead and say, I am leaving now. I will come back in the morning with bread.

*Scent toh badhi acchi lagai hai tune.* What a lovely scent you are wearing, she says. *Kahan jaa raha hai?* Where are you going?

*Dinner karne,* I say. Out for dinner.

*Kis ke saath?* With whom?

*Akele.* Alone. I am lying. I am going out on a date.

*Akele? Kha lega tu?* Alone? Will you eat?

*Haan.* Yes.

*Mujhe nahi le ke jayega?* Will you not take me along?

It has been a while since she asked me—or, if recent memory serves me right, it has been a while since she has wanted to go out with me. Her sweet, inquisitive tone makes me well up.

*Chaliye.* Come, I say, trying to collect my wits.

*Pehle bolta toh, abhi toh main ready bhi nahi hoon.* You should have told me earlier, I am not dressed for the occasion, she says.

*Aise hi theek hai.* This is fine, I say. She is wearing an ugly maxi.

*Abhi toh der ho gayi hai.* It is too late now. She giggles.

Indeed, it must be so late if I have not had dinner with her in years. I feel like such a cruel, heartless son, who has made no effort to bond with his old, fading mother. I walk out almost in tears. I stand in the dark, unlit stairs to take a breath. I do not want to appear worried on my date. Oh, how Mother caught on to that fragrance! It is criminal of me to look forward to a good time when she is suffering.

It is Christmas once again. In the morning, I walk in the pleasant weather to Rabindranath Tagore's house, Jorasanko Thakur Bari. This is the room where he breathed his last: An inscription in Tagore's bedroom welcomes me. It feels like a museum describing a fossil that never decays. Finding myself alone in his room, a geyser of unchecked emotions spring from within me, making my eyes wet. I have found my eternal in my songs, he said in one of his poems. Tagore's house displays photographs of him looking like Tolstoy, Zafar and sometimes just as himself. I decide to walk to my father's office in Macchua Bazar. From Tagore's house, I walk into a dirty lane and confirm with a muri, puffed rice, seller that this is the lane I am looking for. It is where my father had once taken me to his own house.

Standing in his shop after god knows how many years, I see him in a photo frame proudly displayed at the entrance. In it, he is accepting a cheque for flood victims from Jyoti Basu. He can share a stage with the state's chief minister, but not with survivors like Mother and me. The flood in my eyes is about to break the dam. My first instinct is to ask the boy who works at the shop, Is this man still alive? Words sitting at the back of my throat resist moving forward. My teeth can bite them into silence. I ask for directions to the Royal Hotel in Barabazar instead. My father had once filled my palm with coins for firni. Eating the almond-flavoured sweet dish, I can only wish that he is not dead now. My debts I clear in every morsel I numbly swallow.

Since I have come this far, why not visit Bandook Gully? It has been almost twenty years since I left. I climb the stairs to the first floor. I slide my facemask under my chin to catch my breath. The place looks wrecked—empty and soulless. The door to my mother's room is padlocked. It looks tiny. I have read that when you return to your home after a very long gap, everything shrinks. Is it because one has grown up? I might have to lower my head to walk in through the portal. I stand outside the door, taking deep breaths to soak it all in. My feet twitch as if they want to dance. Memories will return if I stare any longer. I look around with the eyes of an orphan.

# 2021

MOTHER HAS A RULE IN HER HOUSE SHE FOLLOWS ALONE. NO daytime TV. We watch TV after 6 p.m. There is a song in the film *Padosan* that goes, *Sharm aati hai magar aaj yeh kehna hoga/ Ab humey aap ke kadmo hi mein rehna hoga.* It loosely translates to, I am embarrassed to say this, but I have to admit that I am destined to reside at your feet.

This song needs to be updated, I say to her.

*Kyon?* Why? She asks.

Which woman in this day and age will want to live at a man's feet? What is she, a daasi, slave, an abla naari, a helpless woman?

*Arre, unn dinon mein.* In those days, Mother says.

Those days are over.

*Tu nahi samjhega.* You won't understand.

I do not want to. Love does not have to be servile. Where is the equality in that? The heroine (Saira Banu) is admiring the hero's

(Sunil Dutt) feet as if she is into paer pooja, a foot fetish, which would be okay if she was *uss type ki*, kinky.

Mother laughs. I am not sure there is a word for kinky in Hindi, but she gets me.

Guess who wrote the song—a man, right?

Haan.

Rajendra Krishan. I google.

He also wrote: *Tumhi meri mandir, tumhi meri pooja, tum hi devta ho*. You are my temple, you are my worship, you are my lord. In that song, the heroine (Nutan) touches the hero Sunil Dutt's feet (yes, again) and sings. What is with this lyricist making women sound so subservient to men? As a poet, he should have chosen his words sensitively and been mindful of projecting women with equality, no?

*Phir kya hona chahiye?* So what should the lyrics be?

Just tweak one word. Say pehlu (side) instead of kadmo, feet. Stand beside the man, why fall at his feet? When a man expresses his love at a woman's feet, it is more about haseen paaon, pretty feet, alluding to her beauty and submitting through it. Here the heroine isn't singing a paean about the man's slender feet—she is putting herself under it.

Mother contemplates. I think there should have been a three-level inquiry into the usage of that word. Obviously Lata Mangeshkar did not object to the word kadmo because she was used to singing about helpless women praying at the altar of the alpha male to rescue them. The writer (also Rajendra Krishan) and director (Jyoti Swaroop) must have explained away the warped situation in some way. One can forgive the composer R.D. Burman for not questioning the lyricist, because he did not want to interfere with the words. Gulzar's free verse was already giving him stressful nights. But just look at how they filmed it.

*Situation hai na.* The situation is such, Mother says. She is fully involved in making her point.

What is the situation? The hero is injured. The heroine, who did not like him, has now come to nurse him and is feeling that her rightful place is at his feet? Strangely, she is aware of her emotions: *Sharm aa rahi hai.* She admits she is embarrassed, but what to do, a man's feet is where her heaven is. Uff. But I must now admit, the song has been stuck in my head. I hum: *Sharm aati hai magar aaj yeh kehna hoga/Ab humey aap ke pehlu hi mein rehna hoga.*

Mother laughs. That was the effect I was aiming for. She has accepted defeat. I may not have been entirely convincing or have managed to alter her perspective, but so long as we are discussing, so long as she feels I am sitting with her because I am truly enjoying the mama–son time, I do not know how else I can be useful to her.

Lata effortlessly lifts and drops the last syllable of the second hoga with such a delicate, light touch of wilful submission that it is impossible not to love this beautiful melody, I tell Mother. The reason I sit with my mother in the evenings and watch old film songs is to engage her. I am hoping her health responds to music as once her body, mind, soul moved to it in magical ways. Music helps her recollect her past. A melody often takes her back to an era, reminiscing fuzzy details about her own life in the kotha. Songs aid as chronology to her memory. For example, she can blurt out a movie's name just by looking at the first frame of a song, such as *Jawaniya Ke Din Dui Char*, before the credits are shown on the screen, which in any case she would have trouble reading even with her glasses on. *Yeh gaana* Holi Aayee Re *se hai*, she informs me. It is a random Seventies' film starring Mala Sinha and Balraj Sahni. Mother remembers it instantly before Amitabh Bachchan can include it in a *Kaun Banega Crorepati* multiple-option quiz question. This song is shot in a kotha, featuring, she further adds, Padma Khanna, with playback by a singer Hansa, who sang only one Hindi-film number. My mother is pre-Google Songpedia.

There is more for the next number that comes up, so a little context before we get there: it resonates with our story.

Writer Khushwant Singh once wrote pithily about Sahir Ludhianvi's gynophobia (fear or dislike of women) and gamophobia (fear of marriage), most likely linked to his mother fixation, saying the poet-lyricist probably drank himself to impotency. Sahir, though romantically linked with several women, loved no woman as much as he doted on his mother, Sardar Begum. She had walked out on her notoriously bigamist husband Fazal Din and raised him alone, inspiring Sahir to write the rousing poetry of *Tu Mere Saath Rahega, Munne* in *Trishul* (1978).

The poem had been marinating in his heart for a long time. It was not until her death that he found the right words to express his mother's feelings. In the film, Waheeda Rehman walks out on her lover Sanjeev Kumar, who marries another woman. Holding her infant, she sings the song, traipsing down a deserted road with tears in her eyes but courage in every stride forward. Her words are woeful but strong. She raises her son in harsh living conditions, and on her funeral pyre reminds him to avenge her tormentor, her husband.

It is a stirring melody, evocative, and perhaps even holds a candle in the wind to the troubled times Sahir's mother faced when her husband harassed them for Sahir's custody after she left him.

*Tu mere saath rahega, Munne*
*Tu mere saath rahega, Munne*
*Taaqi tu jaan sakey*
*Tujhko parwaan chadhaane ke liye*
*Kitne sangeen maraahil se*
*Teri maa guzri.*
*Tu mere saath rahega, Munne.*

Composer Khayyam strings the melody with minimal fuss, using slow-tempo instruments in the background to focus on Lata Mangeshkar's plaintive voice, sung as an elegy at her own funeral. She begins the song haltingly, in sync with the distraught mother's slow steps, and gradually, as the mother soldiers on through strife, her voice rises with formidable strength, echoing a war cry from her ashes. It has a heart-wrenching, cathartic effect.

The song is a powerful bridge that connects the mother–son bonding in film to the relationship between Sahir and his mother. Begum died in 1976. The song was released two years after her death, in 1978. Two years after the awe-inspiring melody, in 1980, Sahir, too, died, burdened with grief.

In one stanza, Sahir spells out how a mother's feelings are trampled; daggers are driven into her heart, eyes and ears. It is this kind of mental torture that she has to endure throughout her life. It must have weighed heavily on Sardar, at a time when it was unheard of for a woman to walk away from her husband and raise a child. The indignities she had to face in the community and society.

*Tu mere saath rahega, Munne*
*Taaqi tu dekh sake*
*Kitne paaon meri mamta ke*
*Kaleje pe pade*
*Kitne khanjar meri aankhon*
*Mere kaanon mein gade*
*Tu mere saath rahega, Munne.*

As the song surges, the words become a chilling reminder of mortality and justice in an unfair world. Lyricist Gulzar and Javed Akhtar have spoken about Sardar's commandeering presence in Sahir's life. Gulzar said her voice boomed through the house. *Woh hamesha unhe daant ti rehti thi.* Sardar was always chiding Sahir in the house. Javed Akhtar said, despite it, Sahir sought her approval in every thought, every word he spoke. The duo fed off each other because they had no one else. Their mutual hatred of Sahir's father glued them together, which reflects in stanzas where she admonishes him to never forget her miseries.

I did not know of the existence of this fierce lullaby until now. Mother turns to me, half-smiling, half-foggy inside her square specs. She says, *Yeh gaana maine tab suna tha jab tu mere pet mein tha.* I heard this melody when you were in my womb. Awkwardly, she laughs and says, *Roxy theatre mein dekhne gayi thi.* I watched this film in the Roxy cinema hall.

I am sitting across from her. I cannot look her in the eye. My tears start welling up. She, too, had walked away from my father, a notorious bigamist, and they, too, had fought an ugly battle for my custody. And to think she was watching this song on the big screen back then when I was a foetus, she was caressing her belly with the gentle words of the stanza:

*Tera koi bhi nahin mere siwa*
*Mera koi bhi nahin tere siwa*
*Tu mere saath rahega, Munne.*

In one stanza, Sahir writes:

*Main tujhe reham ke saaye mein na palne doongi*
*Zindagaani ki kadi dhoop mein jalne doongi*
*Taaqi tap tap ke tu faulaad baney*
*Maa ki aulaad baney*
*Maa ki aulaad baney*
*Tu mere saath rahega, Munne.*

Contrary to the iron gloves Sahir's mother wore, my mother, impoverished greatly by her own unfavourable circumstances, has always said, *Bade naazo se paala hai tujhe maine. Kisi baat ki kami nahi honay di hai.* I have raised you with utmost pride. I have not denied you any comfort.

Maybe that is how I will write my mother's swan song.

We go back and forth, trying new doctors and medications for months to keep her away from dialysis treatment. She refuses it. There is a doctor just off Park Street, an old man who charges an obscene consultation fee. Mother likes seeing him. He is older than her. She feels she can trust his prescription and soothing words. *Doctor Saab, hum theek toh ho jayenge na?* she asks him. Doctor sir, I will recover soon, no? *Rekha ka matlab kya hai, amma?* The dotty old man asks her. What is the meaning of your name, Rekha? This ancient relic is calling her amma. I chortle at their interaction. She shows him her palms and confidently says, *Yeh hai Rekha.* This is Rekha. He draws a straight line on the prescription paper and says, *Yeh bhi Rekha hai, magar iss line mein koi break nahi hai.* This is also Rekha, but there's no breakage in this straight line. She smiles. She understands. He is restoring her faith. Except that he is charging too much, she fusses on her way out.

I try keeping her with me in my rented apartment. She behaves for a few days. She then fights, refuses to eat and bangs her head on a wall to be taken back to her house.

She is hospitalized so frequently that I lose count. Simmi calls me and says Mother is not answering the bell. That irritatingly loud bell that can be heard from a mile away. I am not prepared for the worst. I rush to open her door with my set of keys. She is lying on her bed, frothing at her mouth. Unconscious but breathing. I try pouring sugar syrup into her mouth. She does not respond. Her hands are stiff. Her mouth is locked. The ambulance arrives after an hour-long delay. *Kya karein, sir,* the driver says, *yahan parking nahi hai.* The lane is so narrow that he has trouble parking. *Aur upar se pandemic,* he says. And on top of that, it's the pandemic. I can only sigh and move on. The ambulance comes at a steep price. We lift her in a bedsheet, put her on a stretcher and carry her down the stairs. This is the rehearsal of the fear I have of carrying my ailing mother through a D.H. Lawrence poem. Only this time, it takes more than one person. A rehearsal of the last rites. She is taken to the emergency ward. She is pumped with an injection that brings her back to life as if she were underwater. She takes a long breath, her eyes popping out, trying to recognize where she is. I realize I love her at her weakest, her frailest. She is hard to love when she is free and independent. She is so strong, so tough, so resilient, that loving her seems futile. As if she does not need the mush. As if she is better without it. Everyone needs love. Some are just very good at pretending they can do without it. Like me, who takes after her. She has made me so solid that a hug now, from anyone, could completely annihilate me. But I must not shed a tear. I know it will annihilate her. She will be shattered to see me go weak, frail, helpless like her. The doctor informs me that her present condition is called hypoglycemia. I learn a new word. It sounds as if I am well versed with it when I tell friends or her relatives in Poona about her on the phone. Hypoglycemia. No one is asking me what it means. No one will bother to google it.

I meet and speak to her the next morning. *Aaj naashte ke waqt ek buddha ludak gaya.* An old man died during breakfast today, she says, deadpan, as always. Did you eat? I ask. Haan. Yes, she says. Biscuits and tea. Good, I say. *Subah itna halla macha hua tha.* The place was maddeningly loud and chaotic this morning, she says. It must be when someone dies. If you want peace in the room, eat and keep yourself alive, I say. She is in the ICU because of her morbidly low sugar. She had gone unconscious after her insulin shot yesterday afternoon. She would not have been in the ICU if she had not skipped her lunch. Death is the condition from starvation of life. One should always hunger for it.

*Ek aur*, one more, she gesticulates with her raised eyebrow, about a patient lying on his deathbed next to her. All the more reason you should recover and escape, I reply. She is discharged after a few days. I try to keep her longer, and against her wishes, in the hospital, thinking she gets better care there than I can provide alone. One extra day and she threatens. *Kal mere ko yahaan se ghar le jaana, nahi toh main bhaag jaaungi.* Take me home tomorrow, else I will run away. The nurses laugh. One of them says, *Kaise? Yahaan toh kitna security hai.* How? There is a lot of security here. Mother looks at the nurse and considers her response for a moment. *Bhaagne wala bata ke thodi na bhaagta hai*, she says. A runaway doesn't inform before they run. The nurses swallow their daily dose of laughter pill. She watches television with the nurses and is updated on the latest news. She wants to know when Aryan Khan is getting out of jail. Tonight, or tomorrow, I say. *Accha hai*, she says, *ab mujhe bhi iss jail se nikalo.* Good, now get me out of this jail as well. She becomes indisciplined at home when I am not around, eating paan, gutka, oily puris, mangoes, wafers and soft drinks smuggled in by Simmi. I check on her once in the morning and once in the evening. I use the afternoons to write. But the writing is so often interrupted by my worries about her deteriorating health and weight loss, hospital visits and check-ups that it begins to affect my own well-being. I become irritable. I lash out at her. She cries. I leave her to it. It does not occur to me that I am making her condition worse. I cannot sweet-talk. I will have to fake it. It does not come naturally to me. I have never had the responsibility of another person, let alone a mother who is behaving like a petulant child. In fact, I am behaving like a petulant child. How will we get along? We may need a mediator. Who will play that part? There is no one to help us understand each other.

I keep thinking she should die before me. The world will be far crueller to her if she outlives me.

Her haemodialysis treatment begins. Initially, the doctors use her thigh to make a fistula. Now I thought I knew what the word meant, but it has another connotation. Another time, they make a temporary fistula in her neck. She walks around with a bandage and a catheter hanging out of her neck like it is an obstinate vein that refuses to stay indoors. I can barely look at her. How am I going to feed her? She does not flinch. She does not cry. Her courage, her resilience ... I mean, who can match this level of trauma? She seems to have room for endless pain. Soon, she is operated for a permanent fistula in her hand. The purple bruise on her neck, in healing, looks like a stag beetle glued and gnawing at her flesh. Her body is becoming a landmine of medical explosions. On the final day of the enervating year, I have to put her back in the nursing home. I tell my landlady, who, by the way, is a paediatrician—perfect to take care of my child-mother—that I should be putting my mother in a sanatorium at this hour, when the party season is on. What a wicked fellow you are, I tell you, my landlady says. I try to laugh, wearing the title as a badge of honour. It is a consolation prize for my own perseverance in these rough times.

# 2022

Lata Mangeshkar's demise comes through a radio playing under my window. Her voice is eternally alive. The songs play one after another: *Lag Jaa Galey Ke Phir Yeh Haseen Raat Ho Na Ho*; *Aajkal Paaon Zameen Par Nahi Padhte Mere*; *Rahe Na Rahe Hum*.

Mother worshipped two singers at the kotha. Mohammad Rafi and Lata. They were her constant companions through the radio. When Rafi died, Mother was in Bombay. She went to Bombay Hospital, where he was admitted. She sobbed like she had lost her lover.

The night before the nightingale's death, I say to my terminally ill mother, Her condition has worsened. What do you think?

She has been following the news on Lata's health. I am convinced part of her will die when she hears about Lata's impending death. It will break her. Losing another of her dearest.

She won't survive, Mother says coldly.

Why do you say that? I am alarmed. Didn't you say earlier that she has had the amarphal, the fruit of immortality?

She nods dejectedly.

This morning I read tweets. The nightingale has indeed gone without a chirp. I visit my mother's room, tugging the quilt she is nestled inside. Her face pops out like an owl's head.

She died, I say.

Mother scans me for a fool and pulls the quilt over her face. No reaction. No comment. She goes back to sleep as if nothing has happened. I go to the kitchen to prepare tea for her. After five minutes, I tiptoe back to her room to see if the quilt has the cadence of the rhythmic cycle of her inaudible humming breath. It is the one way I have learnt to check on her without disturbing her. We spend the day quietly listening to radio programmes eulogizing the nightingale's voice.

At lunch, when Mother is tucking into her chicken soup, the radio plays *Tera Jaana Dil Ke Armaano Ka Lut Jaana*. She stops eating. The nightingale sings the words *Koi Dekhe*, following it with a melancholic ae-ae-ae-ae trill that makes her sweet voice bore into our deepest, loneliest emotions. Mother weeps.

Are you crying for her? I ask.

No.

Then?

For myself.

That is how abandoned the heart feels when the songbird flies away. She has taken her time to absorb the tragic news. She feels her time is near. I am reminded of John Keats's poem *Ode to a Nightingale*:

Thou wast not born for death, immortal Bird! ... Fled is that music:—Do I wake or sleep?

Mother's elder sister, Gora, dies in Bhat Nagar on Valentine's Day. Mother does not shed a tear. Someone from the family, a cousin's husband, calls and asks me why I am not using my low-caste surname from my mother's side. As if it is something to flaunt. So I ask Mother, How low are we in the caste ladder? She says we are a nomadic tribe. That is all she knows. She murmurs Dhangar. Her surname, from her father's side, is Tamaich, or Tamaichikar from the Kanjar community. The word kanjar comes from someone who ties a dagger to their waist. The community is from the denotified Vimukta jaati. Other communities do not accept food or water from them as they are Shudras in the varna order. No one previously ever told me about my caste and no one ever asked for it. It was like having a birthmark on a part of my body I could not see—behind my ears.

I have never been aware of my caste until now, although except for once on a train journey a few years ago. I took a train from Dehradun to Haridwar. A man in his late sixties, probably a priest in a temple, dressed in a saffron robe and with a white tilak on his forehead, sat across from me. He had a singular thoughtful expression on his face, as if he was chewing on the strings of time while it preserved him.

*Aap kahaan jaa rahe ho?* he asked. Where are you going?

Surely he knew the answer, but that is how one makes small talk. After confirming we were headed in the same direction as the train, he got his answer.

*Aap ho kahaan se?* Where are you from?

Bombay, I said.

*Naam kya hai?* What's your name?

I told him my name.

*Gotra kaun sa hai aap ka?* Which gotra is it?

My face sank into a double chin.

*Jaat kaun si hai aapki?* Which jaati are you from?

I don't know, I blurted out in defence, and in ignorance. These are questions I do not even know how to translate.

*Poora naam?*

I told him my full name.

*Hindu ho, jaat nahi pataa?* he said in a quizzical tone. You are Hindu but you don't know which caste you are from? It was less a puzzle and more an indictment. Even he couldn't decipher it from the surname.

*Yadav hoga.* Must be Yadav. I then understood what this was about. I may have slipped from the varna ranks. Actually, my father is Muslim, I said, trying to silence him. *Oh, love marriage hua hoga na*, he assumed, adding he could sense it from my unshaved beard. *Aajkal ka fashion hai*, he said. It must be the fashion these days. Love, or look, I could not grasp what he was reproaching.

After the last remark, he went quiet. He could have sounded intrusive if he had asked why I had a Hindu name despite a Muslim father.

Trees were flying past the window, the sun was heading up and warm air was filling the compartment.

*Haridwar kyon jaa rahe ho?* he asked, changing tack. Why are you going to Haridwar?

I gave the standard touristy reply. To see the Har Ki Pauri, I said.

I had seen pictures of the ghat where the Ganga enters the plains. The river has a brilliant emerald tinge descending from the mountains. The water is considered sacred to the Hindus, who believe a dip in its cold embrace has curative benefits. The old man was pleased with my answer. Maybe I was on my way to shedding my father's religious birthmark from my skin. An old man's resting bitch face tends to spout myriad truths. Oh, you will find magic in the waters, he said. The first person you speak to will be an angel to guide you. Remember to try the halwa-puri at Mohan Sweets. I walked from the station to the riverbank. The air was clean, the sun pleasant and the chaos perfectly calibrated to blend in and disappear.

I enjoyed the ordinariness of being nobody in a new place. After observing the musical sounds of the gushing waters, marvelling at its iridescent emerald colour and dipping a toe in its icy fingers, I headed for Mohan Sweets. As I walked away, I watched a boy toss a rope with a magnet tied to it. It pulled in coins from the shallow end. Magic. The salty smoke of deep-frying puris and samosas, shiny orange jalebis, with tea on the side—the classic Indian breakfast had tourists clambering to spot a table.

I stood out and ate at one of the standing tables, where uncles park their toddlers to reserve the space. An aunty with tennis shoes peeping out of her baggy blue salwar stood alone, biting into a hot samosa. She smiled at me and small talk began. She said she was here with her family. They were at another shop behind this one. She wanted samosa and jalebi. I said as little as possible, keeping the chat brief about being advised to eat here. She listened patiently and as she moved away casually after polishing off everything on her plate, she washed her hands at a water dispenser and said, *Koi zaroorat ho to batana.* If you need anything, let me know. She left with a head tilt as goodbye. In Indian culture, one is used to hearing people say that when they are taking your leave. It is a polite offering when exiting a room. No one buys into the rhetorical nature of the offer. She was just being a casual angel.

In the years since, the word 'savarna', or the four forward classes of people, has popped up several times on my social media timeline. Initially, it amused me, as I only associated sajna with savarna. Sajna-savarna is the kotha's only jaat. I guess for me it still means checking the sajna's entitlement before getting ready for him. Savarna has become an irrefutable part of our daily online discourse. It makes us check on our own complacency.

What works for me in a democratic anglophone society will not serve me well in the cow belt, extending to all regions lately. For long I have grazed pastures in disguise as a Gaekwad, 'gae' for cow and 'kwad' from door: cow door. Although, it is still the best bet. To belong to the Yadava clan helps you gain entry into the Kshatriya club. Second in the hierarchy after Brahmins. I have apparently not been doing too bad with my fake surname.

I am now acutely aware of my jaat, that I belong to a Scheduled Tribe from my mother's side (Tamaichikar) and to the Muslim minority from my father's side (Khan). Grandmother was from a banjaran background, possibly a Denotified Nomadic Tribe. Writer Anna Morcom, in her book *Courtesans, Bar Girls & Dancing Boys*, makes a mention of how, unlike for the Dalits, the DNT community never had a leader such as Ambedkar to force their interests on to the national consciousness. That makes me lowest in the order, along with my own personal identity belonging to the queer of caste. Three indelible strikes.

Merit alone has been my jaat so far. If people have been inferring my caste from my fake surname, they are making wrong calculations. As for my class and status, my English-speaking skills have been enough to clear my entry to any upper-class echelon in society.

In fact, I have to now elaborate that with my mother's observation. She was once visiting me in Bombay. She sat on the sofa, holding her lunch plate. She looked me squarely in the eye and asked, *Neeche baith jaaoon?* May I sit on the floor? Stunned, I asked why, what about the dining table? Colour drained from her face. She described how she felt when I visited home for the holidays. I was six years old when I returned from Kurseong. She served me dinner and I nonchalantly asked, Mummy, where's my fork and spoon? Her heart filled up. She told her neighbours, *Phat phat angrezi bolta hai yeh toh.* He speaks so fluently in English. She knew spoon as chammach, but had never required a fork for eating. *Fok?* she had asked me. Where should I sit? I had interrupted her. We did not have a table at home. We do now, in her flat in Calcutta, which I left in 2002, and in all the houses I have inhabited since then across the country, where she comes visiting every few years. She still prefers sitting on the floor to take her meals. *English ne tujhe angrez banaa diya,* she says. English has made you a foreigner.

My strong anglophone education has made me indifferent, to not educate myself and utilize the reservation quota that my underprivileged ST status accords me. The country is regressing to ancient times. Religion is shapeshifting into fanaticism. I may have to rely on magic and angels to survive in the future if I allow this to affect me. I have never hankered for caste politics, simply because in a kotha all are welcome, no one is judged by these ranks. There was a hierarchy among the older generation of deredarni tawaifs, who came from royal patronage and musical gharanas, and bednis, who came from trafficked girls—but that is about it. I am oversimplifying it for the express purpose that this is not an academic text. I am not an expert on the matter. What I do know from my experience is that caste does not spill over to who is allowed into the kotha. No kid is taught about caste. Here, money is the only jaat, paat and saath. Caste and company. Tawaifs passed on their place in the hierarchy to their girl child, but it got diluted as new girls from various low castes entered the profession and mingled freely, sometimes bringing in the crowd, like my mother did, which freed her from the constraints of being marked as an outsider and made the deredarnis and bednis loosen their stranglehold on the profession and befriend her, often enjoying the fruits of her labour and blessing her for infusing vitality into their jaded business. Of course, they secretly envied her, but can they deny that she helped them survive in a trade where their class-conscious status was limiting their reach? Once they knew her, she did not face discrimination of any sort. She did not harbour any desire to be legitimized by the deredarnis formally as a courtesan with their illustrious lineage. Unlike, say, the famous singer Gauhar Jan, originally of Armenian-Jewish-Anglo-Indian descent. Her fame was unprecedented, but her background was not. She wanted to belong to the choudharayins of Lucknow. She requested the singing sisters Bichhua Jaan and Nanuha to adopt her as their daughter in exchange for money and gifts. Why did she do that? A different time, a different calling in the early twentieth century, when royalty was still around, patronizing tawaifs with enormous wealth and comfort. With her induction, she was as privileged as a royal. Gauhar Jan was born in 1873. She attained popularity between 1887 and her death in 1930. All of this is much before Independence. Forty years after her death, new India's new money in the Seventies and the Eighties was not coming from the privy purses of royalty, which was abolished in 1971. It was coming from ordinary shopkeepers seeking entertainment. These men were not coming to the kothas for a lesson in tehzeeb, manners. Where would they apply it in their daily life? They could not possibly be going home after a mehfil, a baithak, telling their mother, sister or wife that they had spent time at a kotha. In the Seventies, kothas were considered brothels. The few tawaifs who were hanging on to their sharafat, decency, as performers, could not fight the stigma, and eventually either made room for the sex worker next door or stepped out and embraced it as the new form of mujra, where skin replaced song in a dance bar.

My school had a common element with the kotha. There was no subject on caste. Kids from all faiths were welcome. We dressed alike and ate the same food; no one was given preferential treatment, whether they were rich or poor. My teachers were Buddhists, who showed us monasteries and churches in the vicinity, but did not ask us to step in and pray or meditate. There was no institutionalizing of any religion. I grew up race, caste, creed and gender agnostic. I cannot deny how it affects the lives of those who are mistreated for it, but for me to suddenly champion it through my own lack of knowledge will come across as insincere and opportunistic, brandishing my newfound understanding of my pedigree.

Four days after Gora's death, Mother and I are back in the ICU. I suspect this is her way of grieving her sister's death. What if I slip into a coma like Hasina, or die of neglect like Gora? I live alone; who will take care of me? She asks, quickly adding, I don't have a daughter-in-law. Violence should have transformed into rage, but I react calmly, with silence. Mother is using Gora Mausi's name to blackmail me. I am so disoriented that I play Wordle in the hospital. I may have been trying to preserve my own sanity.

I don't have money any more to pay for the hospital bills, I say to my mother.

What to do? She turns to me sluggishly.

When one is lying on a bed in the ICU, real life begins to function like an art film, in slow motion. So slow that before she can fully turn to me, the answer has raced across the vacant corridor of my mind in cinema veritè, shouting: Deal with it!

*Do baali hai kaan ki almari mein,* she says. I have two earrings in the almirah. She speaks in a musical cadence, as if it is the lyrics of a shringar ras melody.

I picture it melodramatically. Black-and-white film. No music. Sombre mood.

How much are they worth?

*Dus–pandrah hazaar.* Ten–fifteen thousand rupees.

That won't be sufficient.

*Main yahaan se nikal ke de doongi.* I will pay after I am discharged.

They won't let you leave until you pay.

*Dekha jayega.* We'll see.

*Dekha jayega?* What's left to see? I think.

I have exhausted all my so-called savings. Lakhs have been spent in medical bills. My bank balance is over. I have not worked for two years because I have not had a moment away from attending to my mother. I am this close to begging on the Internet. Should I reach out to a crowd-fund platform for help? Should I ask random strangers on Twitter? Should I become the face of one of those help-us-we-are-poor ads that we soullessly skip on YouTube? I am no less guilty of skipping it, neither pardonable through confession. It takes so much dignity away to beg. Also, how does one help if one lives hand-to-mouth? For some, helplessness is not a situation. It is a condition, a malaise they cannot escape. I find myself oscillating between situation and condition. Mother and I are the only family we have left. I do not know whom to ask. I phone a friend. Yep, that *Kaun Banega Crorepati* line! No questions asked, he promises to help. Situation under control. My house help, in whom I confide, says the poor would rather die with bills mounting like this. I am aware of gleaning even the wisdom of the have-nots, for the half-sighs of the benumbed haves that I am.

Our fortunes are about to change. In this despairing hour, I tweet a photograph showing Mother dancing in the Bombay kotha. It bears a striking resemblance to Alia Bhatt's titular character in *Gangubai Kathiawadi*. The film is just out in theatres. They are both wearing an identical white sari, with a red bindi, dark bangles, earrings and a necklace. What is even more similar is their styling, with their sari's pallu tucked into their kamar, waist, their curly hair in a bun and a youthful appearance that makes them look alike. The tweet goes viral. Several online media outlets pick it up. Mother is in the news. Next I tweet her photo from her hospital bed, about to be discharged. She enjoys the attention. Hello tyooter, she says, smiling for the camera. I have forgotten to get her a change of clothes.

*Kya hum nangey ghar jayenge?* she says. Am I going home naked? This quip is indication she is in a good mood. If we are not going to make money soon, at least she could die famous. This is not my plan. She had once said to me: *Tu meri photo internet pe kyon nahi daalta?* Why don't you put my photo on the internet? What she meant was that unlike most people using social media, I was not uploading her photo as my mother on Facebook. She insinuated that I was embarrassed of her. Which was not true, but I saw her point. I was not being the gushy son she wanted to see. So now I put out more tweets linking her to the Alia Bhatt film. These tweets gain traction and keep me distracted from gloom. One tweet about us not having enough money to pay the hospital bills has a famous actor's wife DM me. She herself is a breast cancer survivor. I guess she understands the dire situation, but I politely decline her offer to pay. The tweets reach Sanjay Leela Bhansali. He wants to meet me. I tell Mother about it. She says to go meet the man. Working with him has always been a dream. She says she will manage.

I take her to a late-night show of *Gangubai Kathiawadi* on Women's Day, along with Simmi and two other women. *Alia se zyada golchakkar toh main kar leti thi,* she remarks on the actress's dance in *Dholida*. I could do more spins in my time than Alia. She weeps when Alia's character is elected girl boss in the brothel; she laughs at the lighter moments. She enjoys the spectacle purely as a form of escapism from the harsher realities of her life, stepping out of the cinema hall to snap out of it in a nanosecond. Film over, magic spell over.

*Jaldi taxi pakad, ghar jaana hai, badi zor ki susu lagi hai,* she says. Get a cab quickly, I have to go home and pee.

I make arrangements with a tiffin-delivery service for her while I am away. Wendy will come every day, I inform her.

Candy? she mishears.

Wendy, I repeat.

Randi? she says.

Oh ho, Mother, you can never say that, please.

*Kaisa naam hai?* What sort of a name is this?

A food rhyme might help her.

*Jaise bhindi, waise Wendy.*

Windy, she smiles.

It is almost settled then, but not quite. There is a new house help she finds mildly agreeable.

Ask her name, I say.

*Kya naam hai tumhara?* Mother asks. What's your name?

Sushmita.

Sushmita leaves her phone on the table and goes to the kitchen. Sushmita's phone rings.

Mother calls her, *Aishwarya, O Aishwarya!*

She has two beauty queens at her service for the price of one. Mother is not trying to be funny. It is her faculties giving up. The offer to meet Bhansali holds promise: It is likely he will employ me in his writing team for his new Netflix series about courtesans. I cannot miss this opportunity. I have to try. I book a flight and humour myself during the turbulence, playing *Dola Re* from *Devdas* as the plane swings to the famous words *Dola re dola re dola re dola.* In 2002, I was playing the songs of *Devdas* on full volume at the kotha. It was soon after that I left the kotha forever. The music of *Devdas* was perhaps the last time the kotha resounded with joy. Oh, sweet irony.

The meeting with the film-maker goes well. I am hired on the spot. I return to Calcutta the next day, happy to report to my mother that I have got the job, my first in four years. I fly back to Bombay in a week. A friend helps me with accommodation. I check with brokers for a flat over the weekend. The filmmaker is not pleased with my work. I am back to Calcutta in less than a month. I am paid for that month. It is enough money to coast us through a few months.

Before I leave Bombay, I meet the singer Rekha Bhardwaj on the eve of my birthday. My tweets have resonated with her. She lives in Oshiwara. We meet at Starbucks. In 2002, when Rekha Bhardwaj's album *Ishqa Ishqa* was released, I listened to the song *Roshni* on loop on a Sony Walkman. I was on a bus trip from Gurgaon to

Ajmer, going to the dargah sharif to tie a dhaaga, a thread string, for a mannat, a prayer. Cut to twenty years later, I am recounting the story to Rekha Bhardwaj in person. I tell her how I was in love with the album, and in love too. It transported me, physically and emotionally, to seek truth, identity and acceptance. The line *Ghar jala liya hai ... haaye* in *Roshni*, at that time, when I was young and raring, felt both rebellious and renunciant. She sang it with so much feeling—her haaye, that sigh of complete dejection of hope, inspired reinvention. I tell Bhardwaj how this particular album, *Ishqa Ishqa*, gave me direction, made me seek solace in chaos. *Dhaaga baandha, mannat maangi,* I say. *Arre wah, phir aap ki shaadi ho gayi?* She asks? After the prayer did you get married? I laugh, take a pause and say, I am queer. Oh, she embraces the information with a smile, and says, *Mujhe pataa nahi tha*. I didn't know. How could she? Because her name is Rekha, and she had easily and readily accepted me, I think of the other Rekha, my mother. I have never had the confidence to tell my mother in these exact words that I am queer, the way I feel comfortable to express it to Rekha Bhardwaj. Maybe it was something pending, since I heard *Ishqa Ishqa* twenty years ago. *Ghar jalaa liya tha.* Her voice gave me fortitude. *Shayad main picchle janam mein tawaif thi*, Bhardwaj jokes. Maybe I was a tawaif in my previous life. Maybe the reason I do not tell my mother is because I can allay her illness by balancing her on the hope that someday I will settle down. But maybe she knows. How long can I pretend to be a saint? A stanza of a Faiz poem in Rekha Bhardwaj's grieving voice reminds me why my mother is my child now.

*Raat mein jinke bachche bilakhte hain*
*Aur neend ki maar khaaye huye*
*Baajuon se sambhalte nahi*
*Dukh batate nahi,*

*Minnat o zaariyon se behalte nahi*
*Unn haseenaon ke naam.*

You did not wish me yesterday—it was my birthday, I say, cutting a slim triangle in a Theobroma pound cake I got from Bombay to celebrate my birthday with my mother.

Oh, she says. But before she can say more, I stuff her mouth with cake. A diabetic would insist on a Giza-size triangle. Her emotions cascade down her food pipe. You should have told me, she breaks a small piece from the cake I am choking her with and feeds me. I choke. How does a mother forget her child's birthday? How does the child remind? After small talk, I leave her house. She stands at the window and says aloud, Bye. I look up and see a frail, ancient woman with feeble fingers, her body shaking as she tries to fix her gaze on me. I cannot be certain how far she sees, but she waves with confidence. I walk into a narrow lane. A hundred men, dressed in white, are standing outside an unpainted, red brick mosque with stained-glass windows. They are humming a naat. A hundred humming sounds create a melody that feels out of the ordinary—pure, powerful but soft, divine even, a celestial symphony, perhaps. Time stops. I walk through the devotional chorus, an apostate passing through a praying field. An old man sprays scented rose water as if tenderizing testosterone. In each of those kohl-lined eyes gazing through me, I lower mine. As I exit the crowd, I feel like I have passed through a prayer. I turn to make a birthday wish. May my mother's memory of me return.

A month later, I blog about my experience working with the maverick film-maker. The blog goes viral. I have to withdraw it within forty-eight hours for obvious reasons, inviting unnecessary trouble. However, Shah Rukh Khan's production team at Red Chillies Entertainment reads the blog. They offer me as a senior script creative position in the company. This news, along with seeing her photo splashed in a recent essay I have written in the magazine *Outlook* about our years in the Bombay kotha, Mother's heart is finally pleased. She tells her friends and neighbours that her son is working for the mighty Khan. It is only now that she acknowledges that I am a writer. Who can deny a validation like Shah Rukh Khan? I am far from working with him, but why burst her bubble? I want to wear my jewellery: haathphool, jhumke, haar and pose for pictures, she says. Do you want to pose like Alia Bhatt? I ask. *Alia se meri shakal nahi milti.* My face doesn't resemble Alia's, she says. I show her a photo of Meena Kumari reading a magazine. We agree to recreate the pose with a similar sari, a long braid and her reading the *Outlook* article. *Meri photo toh bahut chhoti hai,* she says, commenting about the inlay in the essay. But the world is seeing you now, I say. She smiles brighter for her pose. This photo tweet also goes viral. For a while, it seems like good times are kissing our sullen cheeks.

A month after my birthday, we celebrate hers. I want to die, she sobs. Most people want to die on their birthday. They feel it is a grand, enigmatic exit. Die after you see your book, okay, I say. She stops crying. I get her a new kaftan dress, a cake and Rekha Bhardwaj video-calls to wish her. I want to sing a song for you, Bhardwaj says. She is enjoying the chat. Which song should I sing? *Sasural Genda Phool,* Mother says. *Hoye, hoye, hoye!* I can use this moment to convince my mother that we should move to Bombay. The two Rekhas can meet in person. Who knows, we might also meet SRK. It is an idea that I let her think about without pushing too hard. The nurses at the hospital, where I take her for her tri-weekly dialysis session, joke that she should get me married. I will get married, she says. To whom? A nurse asks. To anyone, she says. Aren't you too old for marriage? Asks a nurse. No, she says, my son is old. Another time, she wants to beat the doctor for not discharging her early. Once, she is in the toilet, when I tell her that we are getting late for her session. She steps out and says, *Tatti phans gayi.* Shit is stuck. Where, I ask, naturally not concerned about the non-working flush in her toilet. *Chuttad mein,* she says. Shit is stuck in her arse. I do not know if I should laugh or ask her to go back in and push it out. Now? I ask her for a solution. *Ab kya?* Now what, she says, *Chalo jaldi, sab wahin toh hagna hai.* Let's go quickly, all shit has to be done there.

It is September when I take her to Bombay. On the flight, as I panic during turbulence, gripping the sides, she holds my hand through a cloud. The cloud is a mile long. I think of how tiny she is with her many health issues, and yet she has so much strength. Her grip is soft yet firm, actually just warm as the hand of god. How will I get past this giant feeling I am having at the moment, overcome with emotion, my eyes welling? What did I do right to deserve this beautiful bundle of failing nerves? Her twinkling eyes, her innocent smile—she is the mothership! What do I have to worry about now? The first night in the new apartment in Versova is late-night horror. She wants to eat biryani. I indulge her. She wakes up in the middle of the night, her nightdress soiled. She has managed to find her way to the toilet in the dark, leaving a long train of poo from her bed onwards. I wake up to the noise. Time to wrap a cloth around my nose and clean up. I curse my fate. But I get the work done before the new house helps show up in the morning. Shama and Jyoti, two maids working next door, begin working immediately. Surely, they are god-sent. Even their names match. Both mean light. Much needed into our dreary lives. It is a task getting a house help in Bombay. Housemaids work for a fixed hour and often flit across several apartments in one building. Finding one is usually easy, but a good one is rare.

I find a hospital in Versova for her dialysis sessions. Jyoti agrees to take her while I attend the Red Chillies office in Khar. Mother finds her footing in a month. I spend hours in the evening after work watching her dodder around the house like a toddler learning to walk. I am teaching her how to use a touchscreen phone. She is used to the push-button ones. She wants to upgrade. Her shaky fingers cannot flick the phone receiver icon up. *Chidiya udd,* I say, playing the children's game. She follows my instruction and finally manages to make the icon fly up. She laughs, winning at hello.

She lets out a raspberry tart at dinner. Meaning she farts aloud. *Yeh kya hai?* I ask. What's this?

Paad, she says, matter-of-fact.

*Khaate khaate!* While eating!

*Haan, ab kya karein, paad aa gaya,* she says, Yes, now what to do if it has come uninvited?

An uncommon, if not entirely unpleasant guest at dinner. *Padori,* I whisper to myself. Farter.

*Aaj kaun si film dekhni hai?* I ask mother. Which film do you want to watch tonight? We have just returned from the hospital. She is feeling gay after the doctor said she will be fine soon.

Yakeen, Safar, Do Waqt Ki Roti, Jhoothi *aur last mein* Zindagi. I rattle film names on the Prime Video carousel.

*Zindagi*, she says, beaming.

Another time, she is watching Kaali Kuhi on Netflix. How's Shabana Azmi, I ask. Baad mein bataoungi, she says. I'll tell you later. Bhootni hai ya chudail, I ask. Is she a ghost or a witch? Baad mein bataoungi, she says. Kab? When, I ask. Jab main chudail ban jaoungi, she says. When I turn into a witch.

One weekend, I am at home in the evening, having made myself a gin and tonic, reading David Diop's terse and tense book *At Night All Blood Is Black.* Mother rushes into my room. Montu, Mantu, Manto, she blabs when she panics. *Khoon,* she says, showing me her fistula arm. Blood. She has removed the dressing from her dialysis session before time. Blood is streaming from it. The state of the furry white carpet on the floor you can imagine. I calmly take her back to her room, pat to comfort her and apply a new bandage to staunch the flow. All of this happens in less than a minute, but it is enough for me to go back to my room and feel dizzy. I am going to pass out. It is too much for me. Now I can never forget that book. It will haunt me every time I see the cover. I refrain from putting this incident as a social media post, unlike her other fun stories. This one is triggering even for me.

Friends come to meet Mother on Diwali. She is the star. A hit with our neighbours. Her stories have their own fan following on social media. Once, Shama serves her baasi rotis, day-old rotis, soaked in ghee. She loves day-old rotis like Meena Kumari. *Yeh kada nahi hai*, she tells Shama. This isn't crisp. *Mere ko lagaa tum chaba nahi sakti,* says Shama. I thought you couldn't chew. *Toh kya main buddhi hoon? Chaba nahi sakti!* Mother flares up. So you think I am old? Sorry, Mummy, says Shama. I have trained Shama to call her Mummy in crisis situations. I do not call Mother Mummy, using aap to address her. She calms down if someone calls her Mummy. *Aa, tujhe chaba loon*, mother jests. Come, I'll chew you. *Mota gosht hai mera,* says Shama. I am fat-fleshed. Shama is a witty match. *Kaccha chabbaungi.* I will chew you raw. It is blood for breakfast.

Another time Jyoti asks her, *Aaj kiska birthday hai?* Whose birthday is it today? *Santa Cruz ka,* Mother says. *Kaise manata hai birthday?* How does he celebrate it? Jyoti asks. *Santa Cruz ek bottal pee ke magan ho jaata hai.* Santa Cruz goes merry after drinking a bottle of alcohol, says Mother. *Haan kya?* Jyoti is disbelieving. *Santa Cruz keh ke gaya mera budday pee ke manao.* Mother tries convincing her to drink. Santa Cruz has said to celebrate his birthday by drinking. Jyoti wants proof. *Aisa kidhar hota hai?* Where does this happen? Mother's confident bluff is: *Poore India mein.* Across India. Am still not going to serve her wine, if that is what she is hinting at for Christmas.

# 2023

In January, Mother experiences pain in her lower back. She is unable to rise from her bed. Massage helps mildly. One doctor suggests an expensive injection. Another doctor says to wait. The pain swings between severe to sweet. She wants to use the bathroom. She calls me. I stand at the door of her room, encouraging her to try getting up. She tries. Fails. Repeats. The radio is playing *Uth Meri Jaan, Mere Saath Hi Chalna Hai Tujhe.* Get up, you have to walk with me. I mean, really! What is life without dramatic background music? Sonu Nigam is imploring better than me. *Uth meri jaan,* he sings the refrain. Mother is nearly there. *Uth meri jaan!* I think I will have to interject. *Uth meri maa, bathroom akele hi jaana hai tujhe.* Get up, you will have to go to the bathroom alone. She will run. That helps her immediately.

Another night, I feed her her comfort food—dahi-cheeni-bhaat. *Yeh lo, ek last badaa chammach,* I say. One last big spoonful. *Bahut zyada hai,* she complains. It is too much. *Theek hai, do hisse kar dete hain.* Okay then, two smaller morsels. *Ab yeh kitna kam hai.* See, it's not that much. She is conned into eating more. The radio is playing *Maa Da Ladla Bigad Gaya*. I kiss her forehead. She weeps. She makes me teary-eyed. She knows she is going soon. She does not want to tell me.

*Doctor Saab, main theek toh ho jaungi na?* she asks. I will recover, no? Oh yes, you'll be fine for another five years, he says. She is looking like a shadow of herself. Her eyes hollow, body shaking, she is unable to walk, swallow food or even speak properly. Shama and Jyoti give her a bath. I am in the kitchen when they open the door, revealing my mother, standing stark naked in the tiny space. She turns to look at me. It is written on her face. This is her last look alive. I have seen her ghost, her face white as a phantom flower. Around Christmas, she was opening the door for me, performing a jig with a hearty smile, when I returned from work, singing *Duniya Mein Aisa Kahan Sab Ka Naseeb Hai* along with the radio. I was taking her for a walk in the park. She sat on a swinging bench; her legs swam in the air beneath. She seemed happy with our mother-son time.

On our way back from the hospital after her dialysis session, Mother spots a black cat crossing our path in the driveway. *Kaali billi,* she says, and sits on a bench under a mango tree. I do not believe in superstition.

A friend serves hash brownies at her house party. I return home in the wee hours, a zombie. Mother notices I am sleeping all day. She waddles into my room saying she will fetch a doctor for me. I smile in a daze. Poor woman, mustering up all her strength to look after me. I can only weep seeing her kindness. I am not used to love.

In February, she is lying in bed, releasing one toot after another, a symphony in D-major, perhaps equalling Mahler's *No. 9*. I am only counting by numbers, not rhythm. I tease, asking why she is passing so much wind. *Paad bhi koi rok saka hai bhala?* she says. How can anyone stop a fart? Fair point. I consign it to her good mood. In the evening, I get dhokla and jalebi for snacks after work. A treat. She eats silently, enjoying it. Mother thinks jalebi is my favourite sweet snack. Over the years, whenever she has gotten jalebi for me, she is happier than I am. The next morning, on Valentine's Day, Mother barges into my room at around 7.30 in the morning. *Jee ghabra raha hai,* she says. I am feeling uneasy. She lies down on my bed. She has often complained of jee ghabrana. It is usually gas. A glass of Eno works. It is nothing, I tell her, holding her hand and taking her back to her room. I massage her hands, feet, back, stomach and head. She feels better. Suddenly, she foams at her mouth. I have never seen this before. *Montu beta, main marne wali hoon,* she says. Son, I am about to die. I do not react. Our eyes meet. I do not believe her. She is her most truthful. I should have believed her. I believed my own instinct that she would overcome even this brief pain. I was wrong. I did not react. She looks calm as death. Beautiful, in other words. She is holding on to my face. I wipe the foam around her mouth, saying maybe she should sit up. She agrees. I pile up the pillows against the headboard. She sits back. Do you want water and your morning tablet? She nods. I pass her the water and medicine. I am standing in the room when she takes the pill. Are you feeling better? She looks up at the ceiling. Her mouth opens wide. She drops her head like a nod. I register it as a nod. I feel a rumbling in my stomach. I have to go to the toilet. It is a scene out of *The Marrying Man*, a bawdy Nineties' comedy I recall only for this particular moment. Alec Baldwin's character wants Kim Basinger's character to meet his dying father in hospital. She arrives but finds him asleep or in a coma, I think. She goes to the toilet. The old man wakes up. She returns. He is dead. She misses him by a split second. Death is played out like a shitty gag. I tell Mother I will check your BP in five minutes, okay? Her head remains bent in a nod. I return from the toilet. Seven minutes. I fix the strap on her arm and press the sensor on the monitor. The cuff tightens on her arm; the monitor does a speed reading but drops before the final measurement. I try another time. Still no result. I am strapping her for the third time when I feel her arm drop by the side. Her eyes are not closed in rest. As I had assumed the whole time. She is dead. Maybe at the time I was doing my shit. I check for her breathing. No sign. Pulse. No sign. Shama walks into the room. She, too, senses it. We lay her straight and inform our neighbours. There is a doctor living in the building. He arrives in a few minutes and checks with his stethoscope. I am sorry, he says, she is gone.

My boss from work arrives. Not SRK. That would derail the tragedy into a farce. Perhaps that is what I seek. Anything to remove me from this irreversible personal loss. How will I recover when I am alone? No one recovers from the loss of their mother. No one should. I know what I will be doing for the rest of my life. Grieving. By afternoon, Mother's sister Rohini, friends and relatives arrive at my apartment.

I have to light her pyre. How cruel of me! How can I set fire to this beautiful, radiant, gorgeous woman who looks so peaceful and merely asleep? Mumma! My body shakes. The fire torch enflames my eyes. I kiss her forehead. I cannot watch the pyre burn. I look up at the Versova crematorium chimney scattering her as smoke into the starless night sky. *Chanda ko dhoondne sabhi taare kidhar gaye?* Where have all the stars gone to find the moon?

The next morning we scatter her ashes in the sea. Her relatives perform a ritual of placing a plateful of raw rice inside a sand igloo. It is pulled out to reveal an etching in the rice. It is a flower, a cousin informs me. My mother is telling me from the other side that she is now a raat ki rani, a queen of the night jasmine.

Four days after her cremation, I see her in my dream. She is wearing the camel-coloured trench coat I got for her. The same one Sridevi wore in *English Vinglish*. In 2012, when I was visiting her in

Calcutta, we went to watch the film at the Hind cinema hall. It was a surprise for her. I had not told her where I was taking her. She had not been to a theatre in a decade. *Arre, Sridevi!* She perked up in her seat with a child's glee. She sobbed throughout the film, reminiscing about her visits to my boarding school, nodding her head dutifully and trying to comprehend what the teachers were telling her about my academic progress in a language alien to her. Just like Sridevi. My on-screen mother.

Why are you wearing it? I ask Mother in my dream. *Aise hi,* she says, *koi milne aa raha hai.* Someone is coming to see me. She looks adorable in the snug fit. I kiss her forehead and say, I love you, Mummy. I have not said it in thirty years.

And then I wake up. I cry like a newborn, forcibly wriggling out from the cosmic universe of my mother's nurturing belly.

मुझे याद हो न हो
मेरे बरामदे में
मेरे जैसा
एकलौता पौधा है
जिसे याद रहता है
हर सुबह रात की रानी का
एक फूल महक उठता है
उस नन्हे फूल को
मेरी माँ की तस्वीर में
अपना श्रृंगार फबता है
इसी बहाने मैं भी हर रोज़
उन्हें आई लव यू मम्मी
कहना नहीं भूलता

Whether I remember or not
On my veranda
There is a lone plant
Just like me
The only one
That remembers.

Every morning
A flower of the night-blooming jasmine
Silently blossoms
That tiny bloom
Finds its adornment
In my mother's photograph.

And in this small way
I too never forget
To say every day
I love you, Mummy.

# Acknowledgements

HEARTFELT THANKS TO SWATI CHOPRA, WHO HEARD MY RUNNY-nosed plea for this book over a soothing cup of green tea at the elegantly unpronounceable L'Opéra Salon de Thé in GK2, Delhi, and promptly commissioned it. This book is not sponsored by the tea house, although it's a cosy corner to read in—with a slice of their decadent Vespa-yellow lemon cake.

My agent provocateur, whose name you'll read by the end of this sentence, said that I'd done all of this on my own. Stop it, Anish Chandy! Thanks for your strong and silent character-actor support, though your upcoming role as a playfully shady film producer fits your personality like an indefatigable toupee. Salut!

Special thanks to author and friend Bina Nayak for helping me conceptualize the cover artwork, ensuring that the creases were not smoothed out.

Gratitude to the fourteen women writers who endorsed *The Last Courtesan* and this book at such short notice. You'll find their names sprinkled across these pages. Not mentioning their names here will make your curious mind seek them out like hidden gems, which is good PR.

Thanks to the publisher Udayan Mitra and his infallible editing and design team for facilitating this book. Lagay raho! The proofreader Anju Christine deserves special mention.

Friends, lovers, strangers and even those who exist only in my imagination, you fuel my curiosity to refine, not perfect. Imperfection is the beauty spot.

Thank you to readers of *The Last Courtesan* and to the vatic readers of this book. If you've reached this page, picture me as the dancing emoji.

# About the Author

MANISH GAEKWAD IS A JOURNALIST AND AN AUTHOR. HE HAS reported for Scroll and *Mid-Day*, and has contributed to *The Hindu* and other publications as a freelancer.

His literary works include the novel *Lean Days* and *The Last Courtesan*, a memoir of his mother. He co-wrote the Netflix series *She* with Imtiaz Ali, script-consulted on *Badhaai Do* and served as a senior script creative at Red Chillies Entertainment.

He currently lives online but is scouting for a home address.